THE CHINESE CHURCH
THAT WILL NOT DIE

THE CHINESE CHURCH THAT WILL NOT DIE

by

MARY WANG

with

Gwen and Edward England

HODDER AND STOUGHTON

LONDON SYDNEY AUCKLAND TORONTO

000730

In Loving Memory
of
Pastor Stephen Y. T. Wang

ILLUSTRATIONS

between pages 80 – 81

PREFACE

As a lover of China I lived for many years in the far West, and later I made my headquarters in Shanghai, and then I travelled widely in various provinces. Thus I came to know many Christian Chinese. On returning to England it was my privilege to meet the Rev. Stephen Wang, who had gathered about him men and women whose hearts God had touched. In this way I met Miss Mary Wang, a member of the Council, who is busily engaged in visiting and helping young Chinese nurses in various hospitals, and winning some of them for Christ.

Stephen Wang is now with Christ, but Mary Wang (not a relation of Stephen) came to England, at his suggestion, and at length she has written this book, partly as the story of her own life, and partly as a grim picture of other Chinese Christians who suffered or yielded to Communism.

There are many in England who point to much that Communists have accomplished in China. As Hitler prepared rails and roads in Germany, so Communists have marvellously built new rails and roads in China. . . . But GOD remains, Jesus lives, 'The LORD omnipotent is King!'

Frank Houghton
Bishop.

PROLOGUE

I was born in China. I love my people and my country. I ponder over her great age, her four million square miles, her population of more than 800 million, but she is not too old for me, or too vast, and China has space for all her people. All but those who wish to follow Jesus Christ, who wish to worship Him, and spread His Gospel. For us there is no room. Mao Tse-Tung said: 'Whoever wishes to oppose Communism must be prepared to be mauled and torn to pieces by the people. If you have not yet made up your mind about being mauled and smashed to pieces, it would be wise of you not to oppose Communism. Let the anti-Communist heroes accept this sincere advice from me.'

My family opposed Communism but were fortunate to escape. The elation of those Christians who are in the free world is tempered by the shadow of the relatives who remain in China. Have they been executed or sent to labour camps?

In 1950 there were approximately one million baptised Protestant Christians in China, more than 2,000 ordained Chinese ministers and 10,500 evangelists. By 1966, all the 11,470 churches and 7,500 evangelistic centres in existence when the Communists took over, had been closed. Posters in Shanghai said 'Hang God'. Roman Catholics suffered as severely as Protestants. In Peking the Catholic Cathedral was taken and filled with red flags, banners and pictures of Mao. The church has been silenced but it is not dead. It is even now being resurrected among the twenty-five million Chinese outside China.

My father was the pastor of a church. If he had been a baker or a farmer my story would have been different.

Missionaries brought us the Gospel often at great cost and for more than 150 years Chinese who became Christians were privileged to share that cost. Those missionaries last century who survived cholera, typhoid, typhus and malaria were liable to suffer at the hands of bandits and soldiers. Intrepid pioneers found stoning an almost routine experience. Leslie Lyall has told in *A Passion for the Impossible* how China Inland Mission staff faced death repeatedly, suffering shame and rejection, and incredible hardships. They frequently had no settled residence and were continually on the move, proclaiming the Gospel. In 1877 there was a great famine affecting thirty million people, of whom about one third died, but the missionaries refused to quit.

This century it was commonplace for mission stations to be looted, and there was rarely a year when missionaries were not murdered. You sent your courageous men and women, and but for them we may never have heard of a living Saviour.

Chinese Christians were denounced as 'running dogs of imperialism' before I was born, but they had been taught that following Christ meant taking up a cross. Leslie Lyall tells how in 1938 Christians were attacked by bandits. One woman testified: "During this past year my home has been twice burnt and nothing has been saved. Four out of six relatives there have died, including my brother who was branded with a hot iron. My daughter-in-law was shot through the lungs before my eyes and my only little grandson died of exposure. Yet I will not let go of Jesus Christ. I will not blame Him!"

Mao Tse-Tung has been exalted. His portrait hangs in millions of homes where homage is done to him. To most he is a benevolent figure, the world's greatest revolutionary. Never in history has one single man been so powerful. A Chinese poet puts it:

When the Chairman walks across the land,
The hills and many waters dance;
The Yellow River, tail wagging, chants;
And Mount Omei proffers tribute with open
      hand!

When the Chairman walks across the land,
Workers and peasants joyfully arise;
Hills of grain and cotton split the skies;
Iron and steel in a mighty stream expand!

Mao will die: perhaps before you read these words. But the Chinese church will not die while there remain those who will not let go of Jesus Christ!

I

IT had been a memorable Christmas. Like other Christians in China we had celebrated this festival, had listened to the familiar reading: 'The Word was made flesh and dwelt among us', had sung the traditional carols, exchanged presents, and eaten the special delicacies, but father had been anxious and something of his spirit had conveyed itself to us. 'Wonderful, Counsellor, the Mighty God, the everlasting Father, the Prince of Peace' — nothing could rob the words of their meaning, not even the new Communist regime which ruled our city.

On the night of January 2, 1951, father left our home. We went to bed and he was there. We got up next morning and he was missing. When we asked mother she said he had gone to the country and, at first, I accepted the simple explanation as he often went visiting in the villages, but when he did not return there were more questions, and the Communist officials and the police came knocking on our door.

"Where's the Reverend Wang?" they demanded.

Mother shook her head. She knew, of course, that he was leaving, but had no knowledge of his whereabouts.

"If he isn't here, where's he gone?"

"I don't know, sir, where he is." she replied truthfully, inwardly trembling, but hoping neither to provoke them nor to appear fearful. The strain of recent days had brought on a severe attack of asthma and much of the day she had been in bed.

"He must have told you where he was going. When is he returning?" Their faces showed their distrust, and they repeated the question, now threateningly.

She raised her eyes. "I can't tell you, sir, what I don't know."

My two older brothers, Michael and Martin, and my sister Ruby, were quizzed with myself. Michael knew more than he admitted. I knew nothing. Father had not told me he was going so that I could not be a party to his disappearance. We all shared mother's sickening anxiety, but while we wanted him back we knew it was wise that he kept away. Wise not only for himself but for his family and other Christians in the city.

Father was the pastor of the Presbyterian church, set high on the hill overlooking our lovely city, a large port in northern China, used by the ships of the world. It was one of the most prosperous cities in China, with many fine detached houses with walled gardens. Because of the sea and its lovely location it attracted tourists and holiday-makers. Horse-carriages operated along the sea-front, a few wealthy people had cars; others walked or cycled while the well-to-do used rickshaws. It was a commercial city, with fishing and a naval yard, a few factories on the outskirts, and the best sea food in China. Father had a cycle but often it was stolen.

I was fifteen, not very tall, studying hard in high school, and hoping one day to study music at the university. Both Ruby and I had been encouraged to appreciate music and for me it came next to my love for God and my family. I was proud of my preacher father, with his library of books from floor to ceiling, his quiet wisdom and humour. He might have been a scholar, shut away with his reading, but there were always people seeking him out, and he gave priority to people. Christ had time for those who needed him, and father wanted it to be so in his ministry.

His congregation had grown in ones and twos to more than two hundred, but when the Communists came two years ago it started to dwindle and was now less than one hundred. Nervous Christians were meeting in private homes for worship or finding excuses for non-attendance.

Father was supported by the loyalty of those who remained in the fellowship. His people liked his preaching, the authoritative note, his certainty and his great reverence for the Bible. When his voice boomed out some truth it seemed the walls shook. I liked to see him in the pulpit, declaring and proclaiming, but his sermons were long, very long by western standards. Often he had to eat a meal too quickly or miss it. Preacher's children, like a preacher's wife, have to share. We did not complain. At meal times mother could make a little go a long way, dividing by six, or eight, or twelve if necessary. Mostly we accepted the situations for there were compensations.

Family devotions, with neighbours and friends often joining in, was one of them. The prayers, not always quiet, the Bible passage read a verse each aloud, the lusty hymn-singing, gave a sense of security and belonging, with Almighty God seemingly accessible. I was seven when father first asked me to pray aloud, and my voice no doubt quavered, but it was fear of men rather than of God. I knew the privilege of growing up in a Christian home in China. Only later did I discover the cost.

When the Communists arrived in our city in 1949 there was no bloodshed, no roar of cannon, no bombs, no fighting. Some other cities had air-raids and gunfire, arrests and executions, but with us there was a quiet take-over. The Nationalist soldiers who had been there to defend us were withdrawn and the Communist soldiers came. They took up positions outside important buildings but inside routine continued with little change. The Civil War in China was renewed in 1946, and from then the Communists, many armed with Japanese weapons, gradually took over. Ours was one of the last cities in the province to be captured, and the wealthy land-owners and businessmen had already left for Formosa-Taiwan, transporting whatever they could. They could not take their lovely houses, so they endeavoured to sell them and buy gold, but buyers were not plentiful. Some prosperous members of our church went and few blamed them for all knew what would happen to their possessions when the Communists came.

For several reasons father was advised to move with his family, but he would not consider it. Stories of persecution and imprisonment reached us from various parts of China, but father declared he had never been involved in politics. So we stayed. When the soldiers were within sight of the city we closed and locked the gate in front of the church forecourt and went indoors. Everybody stayed at home, for to be on the streets was to attract attention and most wished, temporarily, to be invisible. When the change in leadership had taken place a majority philosophically accepted it with either patience or indifference.

Father's loyalty was to God but he showed respect to the Communists. They came and paid courtesy calls on prominent and influential families, and the soldiers at first acted with greater consideration than is normal with occupying forces. They moved into the houses vacated by the owners who had fled, were polite to the neighbours, and showed respect to the old. In China we have always respected the elderly, and the Communists cleaned their homes, tidied up their gardens, and placed large notices around the city which read: 'Communists are our teachers'; 'Communism shows us the way'; 'Communism is our hope'. Some believed, a few became fanatical, others, oddly, complained that soldiers did not act this way.

Communism, we were told, would increase food production and there would be an end of famine. Parts of China would be industrialised and would supply the world's markets. Diseases such as cholera and typhoid would be conquered and peasants would share the living standards previously known only by landlords. Education would be for all and new universities would be created.

Their take-over was all the more effective because they did not act in a brutal or loathsome way. Neither bullets nor corruption were evident, and the planes which circled, dived and re-formed overhead were a reminder rather than a threat. It could not and did not last. Father purposefully continued his ministry.

Until 1950 missionaries from America, England and other countries, were allowed to stay, but when the Korean war started the propaganda against them multiplied. The Chinese were supporting the north Koreans and feelings ran high against the Americans. Some were given twenty-four hours to quit the country, others were instructed to apply for exit visas and then kept waiting months.

We were sad to see the missionaries go. One or two were to remain for several years. Miss Helen Willis, who ran the Christian Book Room in Shanghai, whom I was later to know, remained until April 25, 1959. The missionaries had been part of our life; they had preached in our church, eaten at our table, and some were almost members of the family.

Father saw it as his duty as a Christian to be at peace with all men. At first the kindness of the Communists convinced him that his non-involvement with their politics was right. Later he saw how they were indoctrinating his people and he realised that Communism and Christianity could never make a partnership. The Communists believed Christianity was a tool of western imperialism used in aggression against China.

Each Christmas father prepared a calendar to give to members of our congregation. There was a mailing list of friends outside the church who also received copies. He prepared the 1951 calendar on the theme *Facing the Cross*.

17

There was a picture of the back of Christ, showing him making his way towards the cross. He sensed that 1951 was to be a year of suffering for the church and he was burdened that all should be prepared for it. *Facing the Cross* burned itself upon his heart.

Our church was well-sited and shortly before Christmas the Communists asked if they could borrow it for the district meeting. It seated more than any other building in the locality. The Communists held frequent meetings: those who did not know how to read were gathered together each day so that the newspaper could be read to them. Everyone was grouped to read newspapers, but there was only one kind of news, only one kind of opinion. Young people were organised in the schools, and the smallest children in the nursery knew about Chairman Mao. Older women and housewives and retired people met in the evenings for beween one and two hours. Communist leaders chaired the meetings, and all were asked for their opinion, no one being allowed to remain silent. If a wrong opinion were expressed the person was criticised or ridiculed. It was polite and friendly until one voiced a wrong sentiment, or asked the wrong question and then one was in a wretched and lamentable situation. It did not assist to declare one had no view.

I was with father in his study when the Communists requested permission to see the church. Outwardly he did not flinch, but it was a request he had feared for the church was sacred ground. It was meant for worship and within its walls there was peace and beauty. Their visit was a nightmare.

"You may borrow it," he said slowly with a heavy heart, stepping into a world of darkness and danger, "but please, sir, respect our premises. Remember it is a church. I make two conditions. First there must be no portraits or flags put up because in our church we never put up a portrait of anyone, not even of Jesus Christ. The second condition is that there must be no smoking. It is a church."

"Why do you object to pictures? They can do no harm and it is our practice . . ."

"In our church we do not worship any image. Sir, do as I wish."

"It will be so."

The speech had been courteous. Father knew that his deacons would support him in the view that the new regime should not be unnecessarily offended. They bowed slightly and mentioned their gratitude. The meeting was to be on the evening of the day after Christmas, December 26.

"I wish they hadn't asked," he said to himself again and again. "Did I do wrong in saying yes, or was I right to avoid unpleasantness?"

He brooded on it as we celebrated Christmas. The bells rang out, and the stars shone brightly in the cold night, and we heard the story of Mary and her child Jesus. 'Peace on earth, goodwill towards men' — that was part of the Christmas message. He needed the wisdom of the Wise Men, but they came after Christmas.

In the afternoon on the day of the meeting, about 3 p.m., he was informed that he was required at the police station for a talk. While he was at the station those responsible for the meeting arrived to prepare the church. When he returned the meeting had started and he was told that the portrait of Chairman Mao had been hung between the flags. His informant added that members of the audience were smoking as they wished.

The house of God had been desecrated. He called the family together and we went to his study.

"I want you to stay here," he said, "and pray. I will be back shortly."

He did not tell us what he was going to do, but the tone of his voice and the serious expression on his face worried us. He found a small ladder and took it into the church. There was a low murmur from the stunned audience as he walked to the front and took down the portrait of Chairman Mao and removed the flags. No one restrained him. He left the church unmolested. Outside he exclaimed: "I expect my principles to be respected."

He returned to the study still looking very serious. "I have done what I wanted to do," he said. "I have removed the portrait and the flags. They did not keep their word."

The tone of the Communist meeting in the church changed. Instead of a talk the audience were encouraged to shout slogans requesting that the Government punish Pastor Wang because he had insulted Chairman Mao. An uneventful session had become a high-powered propaganda event. Father would have to pay for his action, but mercifully God reveals the future to us in single days.

Two days later, I was alarmed at a meeting in the Town Hall, which I was attending as a representative of my school. The speaker said: "Among the religious leaders in this city, among the pastors and the missionaries, there are bad elements, wicked men who do not respect our Chairman or his leaders, and do not honour our flag. In our new liberated nation it cannot be permitted."

I knew then why I had been selected to attend this meeting as a young delegate. At school I was regarded as backward concerning the revolutionary thinking and so I considered it strange to be chosen for this supposed honour. Others in the audience knew that the speaker was referring to my father removing the photograph and the flags, for news of the incident was now known throughout the city.

Should I tell father? I kept asking myself as I went home. I did not wish to add to his burden. For days he had hardly spoken. Facing the cross, facing the cross, was the theme in his mind, but I was concerned for his safety. He paced with a restless dignity, his face more set than I had ever seen it. Deciding he should be warned, I burst out what had been said. He was uncomfortable but anxious only to reassure me. "Do not worry. I am not that important. They may be more trustworthy and honourable than we think."

"Father, I hope so." I could not conceal my alarm. It was unbearable to think that anything might happen to him. "I really hope so."

He looked at me and his face relaxed. There was tenderness and concern for me in his voice. "God understands. Let us talk to him about it." Behind his words and his smile I could sense his anguish.

It was the last time just the two of us prayed together for seven years and I was to recall it.

On December 30 at the university where he was studying, Michael heard a broadcast. It was a recording of the confession of a man who had been shot the previous day as a counter-revolutionary. In the confession he mentioned father. Michael knew that the confession had probably been forced on the unfortunate man and that father was being framed.

On January 1 a meeting was convened in the Y.M.C.A. of church representatives. It was arranged by the Communists to prepare anti-American propaganda for use in the churches, and to foster support for the north Koreans. A second aim was to identify those church leaders who were unpatriotic, failing to love and honour China. Father, as chairman of the local union of churches, had to be present, as did Michael, representative of the university Christian union. A Communist official addressed the meeting and he mentioned father as a counter-revolutionary whose influence was harmful. The government, he said, expected church leaders to deal with him.

Michael was warned that it was planned to call a mass

meeting of all the Christians in the city on January 6 to accuse father. The meeting was to be in the park. Leaders of selected churches had been approached and told that they must publicly accuse him. If they refused they too would be suspect.

The speaker mentioned ten charges against father. The root of these was that he had served as a pastor during the civil war, the Japanese war, and at all periods, thus revealing a basic disloyalty to his country. As a Christian leader he had shown respect to each different authority and this demonstrated his guilt.

The pastors who were to prefer charges against him came to Michael to explain their dilemma. If they refused they would be in trouble. They wanted to find a way of saving him without exposing themselves.

An unbelievable plan was hatched. When father appeared on the platform at the mass meeting someone would step forward and violently injure him so that the trial could not take place, and his accusers would be prevented from giving evidence. Michael was asked to co-operate. When father had been injured a member of the family would step forward and request that he be allowed to go home to be nursed. This to avoid his imprisonment. The injury must be genuine.

Michael, deeply disturbed, demanded time to think. On January 2 he went home from the university and told father of the predicament of his fellow ministers. There was one honourable thing to do, Michael urged, and that was for him to leave the city.

A family photograph was taken. Two relatives arrived and their presence suggested important family decisions. I was uneasy. After we went to bed their talk continued into the night. It was difficult to sleep, for our home was no longer a place of security, and the New Year held no promise for those who were Christians.

At the photographer's we had smiled when we were told. It was to be a priceless picture for that night father left the city. He hardly knew where he was going, but he did know it was too dangerous to catch a train from the city station.

2

GRANDFATHER, a poor tenant farmer, with little education, died when father was still a boy. Chinese peasants were often in the hands of moneylenders who were also their landlords, but they loved their land and lavished their care upon it, although often the soil was poor. Rice and wheat were the country's staple food, but there was insufficient to meet all needs so many poor people ate only vegetables and porridge made from grains. In season there were various fruits but very little meat. Tea, in everyday use since the eighth century, and boiled water, were the national beverages. Sailing junks brought regular supplies of fish, but this was usually beyond the purse of people like grandfather.

There were bandits loitering in the hills, and much lawlessness and political unrest, but most villagers were just, honest and remarkably longsuffering considering the oppressive taxes, rents and poor markets. If they had dreams they were of bigger crops and elementary education for their children. Although China was one of the first centres of civilisation, life was rural and medieval.

When father was fourteen, the year he became a Christian, he had his first opportunity of serious schooling. Enough money was found for him to have one term at a Presbyterian mission school, five days walk from home. He took some dried food for the journey and slept under the stars, the distant horizon filled with promise of a better life. He absorbed knowledge like a starving man, grasping every morsel, but at the end of his term his schooling finished. There were no more funds.

What could he do? If his mother could borrow some

money he might later repay it. He spoke to her, hesitantly, a bit embarrassed, and she agreed to ask a friend. Three times she went and three times she returned without the loan, too shy to make the request. On the fourth visit she returned flushed with success. It had cost her a great deal, but her reward was her son's joy, the glow on his face!

My father was a good pupil, his mind alert and retentive, determined not to spare himself, and he achieved good marks, so that at twenty he became a teacher. When his future looked secure he heard the call of God to the ministry, which meant further education. He was accepted for specialist study at a theological college. The normal course was four intensive years but his was spread over six so that he could spend half of each week working to support himself and his mother. He did a variety of jobs from assisting in the library to cutting the stencils for printing text books.

Father was rarely separated from his mother. She went everywhere with him. As a girl her feet had been bound which meant that she could not walk freely, but father gladly carried her.

When he had completed his theological training he was invited to remain as an assistant lecturer. Later he studied for a further year at Yenching University, Peking. At the conclusion of these studies, at thirty-three, he was married. It was a time of ferment. To the three Chinese religions, Confucianism, Buddhism and Taoism, the missionaries had added Christianity, but now Communism was invading the minds of men, competing with and threatening all that had proceeded it. Father did not take the threat too seriously, being more concerned with his appointment to the Presbyterian church in the city where I was born in 1935. Nine children were born, but five died, leaving my two brothers, Michael and Martin, my younger sister, Ruby and myself. Until recent years the death-rate in infancy in China was alarming by western standards, but this was accepted like drought and storm. There were no drugs, pneumonia took a heavy toll, resistance hitting its lowest in the winter.

I was four when my eighty-six-year-old grandmother died. She had been a cherished part of our home, the heart of our family and the centre of all activity. Father, constantly sensitive to her need, always went to her room before he retired to bed. He was compelled, not through a sense of duty, but because of the place she occupied in our affection.

In the Chinese tradition she and my eldest brother shared a room, each with a cot on opposite sides, for the first-born son belonged to the grandmother. Although she could not read she learned long Bible passages through listening to father, without whose affectionate care she would have died before I was born.

I did not understand about death. In the morning I went to her room and found her face covered with a cloth. She was wearing exquisitely embroidered new shoes. "Why don't you get up?" I asked, but there was no reply, and as I looked at the shoes peeping below the covering I knew something was wrong for she had never worn such lovely footwear before.

"She has gone to be with Jesus for a long, long rest," father explained. There was emotion in his voice. "She has worked so hard looking after us."

Women from the church came to our home to shed a tear and talk as they made the funeral robes from rolls of white linen. A lorry arrived with a bench on both sides on which the family sat, the coffin balanced in the middle. Four more lorries, all with benches lined with mourners, followed. I went half-way and then returned. Grandmother had done with the body, with its frailties and limitations, but there was a sure and certain hope of seeing her again.

26

When father came to our city there was no church building waiting for him, but he was joyful and confident and full of high enthusiasm. For two years on Sunday afternoons he preached in a theatre, challenging those who came to give so that they might have their own building for worship. Out of their resources, so limited, they gave generously. Stone by stone the new church was built, a cross, the symbol of the Christian faith, on top. Because he was in charge of every planning detail, because it was a visible evidence of a young pastor's faith, it had associations which made him enter its doors with a sense of destiny. No church, however rich in history, however magnificent, whatever its size, could give him more delight. He encountered difficulties, prejudice, poverty, but with a slender young woman as his wife, whose sweetness and innocence had melted his heart, and soon with the makings of a family, hope possessed him.

As the pastor's children, naughty and irrepressible as any children, we were allowed to attend the mission school, of which he was a trustee, without paying. This was a great privilege when most Chinese received little education. Schooling opened so many doors, but we also wanted education for its own sake.

The nation was at war with Japan, and Chiang Kai Shek was in constant strife with the Communists. Chiang told his people: "China has a vast territory, an enormous population and rich resources, and the more extended the field of battle, the more divided will Japan's fighting power become. The enemy will be forced to fight in a manner favourable to China's tactics."

It was nearly true. The Japanese, who had harassed us so long, occupied our city for several years. There seemed so much space in our country. Japan has the highest concentration of people per unit of arable land for any country in the world. Its cities are jammed to bursting. When they took over ours we saw their soldiers on our way to and from school and they moved into the houses in our neighbourhood. Life was much better for them in China, where as occupying forces they were more privileged than in Japan.

Father taught that as Christians we should love all men equally regardless of race or faith, or whether they were oppressors or comrades. It was a high standard. The Japanese children could and did strike us and we were not allowed to retaliate for fear our parents might suffer.

Lin Yutang has written of the Japanese rape of Chinese women, the execution of individuals, burning of surrendered soldiers in closed sheds or by pouring petrol over their heads, of the bayoneting of babies, shooting of civilians in water and the sinking of fishing junks. I did not witness these things: I do not question them, but I do recall the Japanese as prodigious workers, gifted and inventive. They could be both polite and inconsiderate, disciplined and permissive. A small Japanese church was started in the city and the minister became a close confidant of father's and a welcome visitor to our home where he browsed among our books and chatted with us. He was a good man of great learning, an historian.

When I was seven father had malaria. It seemed he was going to die. Methods of treatment now known and readily available might have quickly saved him. We gathered round his bed knowing we could not spare him.

"I have four children," he said. He spoke with dignity although he was sick. "Which of you will continue in my steps and be a preacher?"

No one replied. He asked Martin. "Would you be willing?" He said nothing. Father sighed then simply prayed: "Then God it is not my time yet, please spare me."

"Which of you . . .?" Years later, when I had left mainland China, and knew freedom, I could hear him repeating

28

the searching question as I considered what to do with my life.

A Japanese lady doctor and her husband came to our church and the lady asked if she could examine father. We did not trust her, but she was so insistent that we finally agreed. Surely his ministry was not yet complete: we could not bear the thought of losing him. The Japanese doctor had the drugs father needed and she brought some rice, almost the first rice I had. It was mouldy and needed washing, but who cared? Mother almost counted the grains and made it last several meals. Father slowly began to recover.

During these years of occupation, life was unquestionably grim. Our home was like an inn-keeper's with constant arrivals and departures, extra places for meals and several sittings when space was limited. Missionaries, unable because of the world war to return home, were very welcome. Among my favourites was the Reverend Davies, an elderly American Presbyterian, a widower who had taught father in college. He stayed in our home whenever he wished, spoke perfect Chinese, and in a mysterious way always seemed able to produce cakes and sweets. He thought like a Chinese, wore our clothes and rarely went on furlough even when life was normal. His daughter died as a girl and perhaps that is why he treated us with such kindness. He died in China, after the arrival of the Communists, and was buried on the campus, father conducting the funeral. By request on the tombstone there was no name simply, in Chinese characters, the words *God is love.*

Few churches could afford the luxury of a caretaker, so it was the preacher's children who cleaned the church, and dusted the seats each week. We complained, being normal children, and asked why it should be so. Father did employ a messenger to deliver his letters on a cycle. With encouragement the messenger read and studied to better himself and passed the coveted examination to become a postman in Shanghai. Father little realised that this post-man, in his new location, would be able to assist him in his escape to freedom.

The Christians brought Christmas to China and the children of non-Christian parents were only too happy to join in the festivities. We had a Christmas tree with decor-ations and small presents such as bags of peanuts and dried fruit and new clothes made by mother. There was magic in the air on the night before Christmas when Father Christ-mas distributed sweets to several hundred children who listened attentively to the Bethlehem story. The angels with their song, the shepherds with their adoration, the wise men with their gifts, became part of our lives as we gazed in our imagination on the Christ-child.

We were allowed to sit up until 2 a.m. munching our peanuts. Auntie was always generous. Father had paid for her to have schooling with the result that she was able to take up a rewarding profession: but she believed in useful presents, pencils or exercise books for school — what we would have chosen. However drab and cold the weather Christmas was a warm, cosy time: the Light of the World had illuminated our home.

It was father's ambition, frequently stated, that I should be able to play the hymns on the church piano. When I was nine he took me to the piano teacher's home but long before that I heard him say that one of the greatest regrets a woman can have is not to be able to play the piano. When mother married she was encouraged to take lessons for a year.

My music teacher and her husband were Koreans. He was a pastor of a Chinese Christian church and father had assisted him with practical help and counsel. Now his wife offered to teach both my sister and myself without pay-ment. Father could not have been more grateful.

As we walked to her home, it took about thirty minutes

with me trying to keep pace with father, he confided his hopes.

"This will be my pride if my daughter can play in church for the services, so that I will not need to beg anyone else to do so," he said. I doubted if I would ever be able to accept such an enormous responsibility and I was frightened that the music teacher might decide that I had not even the ability to learn.

It was a lovely piano and I was helped on to the stool. My feet did not touch the floor, but after some finger exercises which were apparently more important than the length of my legs I was accepted.

It was the start of a new discipline. On most days there was to be one hour's practice on the church piano, and excuses, easily created, were not readily accepted. In the summer it could be pleasant, but in the winter it was icy cold and I had to hold very firmly in mind the vision of one day playing for the services. Music, the chiming of bells, good singing, were part of the Christian heritage.

I was eleven when I was given my first opportunity of playing for a church service. There was plenty of advance notice so that I could practise the selected tunes: it was both an ordeal and a triumph. We were a musical family. At family devotions father would glance at the music book and start up a hymn in the right key. Both brothers sang well and Martin played the trumpet.

The Chinese have an intense love for music, painting and poetry. We delight in colour and design as is evident from our calligraphy. I also loved story-telling and as a child I would gather all the children on the steps leading up to the church and tell them stories from the Bible. To us Abraham, Moses, Daniel and St. Paul had Chinese faces: we pictured them in the attire we wore, speaking our language. Over and over I would tell of their adventures and my young audience never seemed to weary.

On the ground around the church were several small homes for families who had nowhere to live. They were extremely modest but some families remained for years paying a nominal rent. We lived in the basement underneath the two-storied church. On the ground floor were the Sunday school rooms, used as nursery classes in the week. The church was on the first floor. For years our home consisted of three rooms, a kitchen and storeroom, but later we were granted additional accommodation.

At the end of the Second World War, in 1945, the Americans arrived and the Japanese occupation ended. The Japanese were counted and numbered and put on ships for Japan. We were not sorry to see them go, but they were reluctant to return, hating leaving the homes they had confiscated. After their surrender they bowed when we passed them in the street; in my heart pity took the place of hatred. They feared they would have nowhere to go on arrival in Japan and stories circulated, most probably untrue, that on the journey some threw their children overboard.

For us it was the dawning, we believed, of a promising new era. The Americans liked our city and we welcomed them and their open-hearted generosity. The last of the Japanese departed and we knew what it was to be free. The gloomy years belonged to the past. No other nation was now our master, the future was ours to chart.

Our war with Japan had started in 1937 and this, combined with the civil wars, had left our country physically desolate. Literacy outside the towns was five per cent. Eighty-five per cent of the population was engaged in agriculture, but tools were of wood as iron had been unavailable. There was widespread malnutrition but we saw ahead a new era.

For the first time I saw a negro. I looked again. China's doors were opening, new growth and development were ahead. Food became more plentiful in the shops. There had been months when the only food was sweet potatoes sliced and dried and later steamed. They were hardly ever fresh and if they were too mouldy we would boil them. Through an inadequate diet father's health had suffered and in 1943 a bad ulcer on his back had caused anxiety, but church members, getting any small luxury, honoured him by bringing it to our home as a gift. I had seen mother's tears fall into the food as she prayed, "Oh God, how long will this last", but with the allies came fresh appetising supplies on an unprecedented scale.

Our city was filled with a new bustle. The Christians hoped that the Gospel would spread like a great wind among China's millions. The Communists planned a revolutionary transformation. Mao Tse-Tung's poem expressed his urgency:

> So many deeds cry out to be done,
> And always urgently.
> The world rolls on,
> Time hurried.
> Ten thousand years are too long;
> Seize the day,
> The hour!

3

WITH the Americans came the Evangelists, practised in publicity, thinking of mass meetings, totally committed to reaching every man. Michael, in his first year at university, used his gift as an artist to paint colourful posters which were displayed around the city inviting young people to a Youth for Christ Crusade. Although my parents had not forced me to the point of decision, believing they should allow the Holy Spirit gently to bring me there, I was concerned, at eleven, about the spiritual state of my friends.

The Youth for Christ meetings were held in a prominent church in the busy city centre, and on a Friday night in July I invited two schoolgirls to accompany me. I wanted them to become Christians. The preacher was Bob Pierce, founder of World Vision, and we found seats in the central body of the church. If the approach was American his preaching came over powerfully and persuasively through an able Chinese interpreter. His text: 'For God so loved the world that He gave His only begotten Son that whosoever believeth on Him should not perish but have everlasting life'. It was not the first sermon I had heard on that text, but like so many preacher's children I had almost stopped listening. I needed to hear a new voice.

There was a responsive congregation, almost all young people, and I had a companion on either side. Throughout the sermon I was praying hard that they would respond to the invitation to follow Christ. I had seen, two nights previously, a thoughtful crowd of teenagers go forward.

The sermon was not for me. The preacher was on target for my friends, but said nothing I did not know, that father had not repeatedly said. I was a daughter of Pastor Wang.

But when the invitation was given I felt the urge to respond myself and I had an uncomfortable feeling that this came from God.

"But I am a Christian," I told myself. "I do not need to do that." The compulsion remained. "It would be showing off, and anyhow I am shy."

"Go forward. Throw away your pride."

"God, you can't really want me to do that. I can confess my sins where I am. How about my two friends? They need changing. Their background does not compare with mine. It is for them I came tonight."

Christ's words came to mind: 'If you will not confess me before men I will not confess you before my Father which is in Heaven'.

I found myself standing up, as my own need dawned in my heart, edging along the seats, hoping those around had their eyes closed. I went forward. There were already fifty or sixty at the front. I went to a corner on the right hand side and knelt down. There were footsteps behind and my two friends joined me. They had followed me to Christ. I prayed for myself:

"Lord Jesus, I thank you for your salvation. I want it to be mine. May I be clear I am a Christian not because of my father, but through my own choice. Make me your loyal disciple, no matter how difficult.

"Make me faithful, God. I will be a Christian all my life, whatever the cost."

I was to remember that vow, but that night and in the following year it was not costly for me to follow Christ.

The Christian churches flourished, congregations being swelled by those who had not been inside a church during the Japanese occupation. American aid was dispensed through the Christian community and added to the numbers. The churches had some of the best schools: food and education are powerful incentives, but father preached the faith rather than analysing motives. He dreaded the coming to power of the Communists for he knew what had happened to the church in Russia.

He was not at the Youth for Christ gathering having a meeting with his deacons and elders, but Michael and Martin were there. I went home knowing it would be easy to tell everyone except mother and father. We Chinese are reticent and build walls around ourselves. I cannot remember when I did tell father but I recall his quiet joy: with mother he had fervently prayed for the conversion of his children.

I worked harder at school. That seemed to be part of my faith. Father while warning against pride said that we should do our best, one hundred per cent, for God. Whether we came first or last was unimportant if we had given our utmost, but he hoped that we would gain a high school placing.

I was thirteen when the Communists captured our city. It was an undramatic event, but cities like men's hearts can be taken silently. At first Youth for Christ continued, and church services remain unchanged. The Communists regarded Christians as unimportant and harmless. We had no priority on their agenda, just children and old ladies they imagined, but when they had the government of the city secure we came under scrutiny and what they saw displeased. From inland towns and villages came stories of executions. Christian ministers were warned to be patriotic by refusing aid from capitalist countries, to be loyal to the new regime, upholding it in their sermons and conversation. Chairman Mao was to be upheld and proclaimed.

Life was tough for Michael at the university. He was involved in many activities, and this was approved, but not his alliance with the Christian students who were fearless in declaring their faith. He was elected vice-president of the students' union, and was also on the management committee which represented both students and staff and was responsible for administration. He refused however to belong to the Youth League or to have any political involvement, wishing to be free, but considerable efforts were made to gain his support for the Party. His professors and tutors advised, "Michael, you must watch for your future. If you will follow the leadership of the Party you can have a better future than any other student. If you don't then your loss will be greater than anyone else's."

Threats followed: "Michael, your refusal to accept the leadership of the Party suggests that you have other associations which might be dangerous. These must be eradicated."

The bribes and threats alternated for one and a half years.

Books of instructions were thrust upon him, to be swiftly replaced with further volumes as soon as he had read them, but this was no ordeal as he adored reading. A strange medley of voices penetrated his mind: some were easily rejected, others held more appeal. It is an old Chinese proverb that the eye-gate is more important than the ear-gate. It did not have to be repeated to the Communists. The first Protestant missionary to China, Robert Morrison, knew the value of the printing press, preparing a new translation of the Bible, a Chinese dictionary and several other books, but for most missionaries the spoken word held greater appeal.

One author, Mr. Y. T. Wu, influenced Michael's thinking creating conflict and confusion in his mind. It was frightening to see him begin to change under the influence of Satan's inkpot. Communism was not only anti-God. It had a blue-print for revolution, and Mao made some observations that none could deny. "What is the most precious thing on earth? It is man," he said. "Our people are poor and blank but the most beautiful poem can be written on a blank sheet of paper."

June 2, 1950, was the first anniversary of the Communist takeover of our city. The university planned to celebrate with a meeting for more than one thousand students and associates and Michael was invited to be a principal speaker. It was strategic, as his father was a minister, for all to know that he had lost his faith. His lecture was to last one hour and would show how students who had initially opposed Communism now welcomed its benefits. Mao himself had been a student and an intellectual, but he had changed himself. "The Revolution," Mao said, "brought me into the ranks of the workers, peasants and soldiers, gradually I became familiar with them and they with me. It was then a fundamental change occurred in me." Michael was briefed, his advisers going over every line, every word, until the speech was exactly as they wished. The content, he was told, was confidential and could not be discussed with anyone.

During the period of preparation he came home from the university on Sundays for the church services. He was respectful to father, but he questioned in his mind what was said, yet was anxious neither to offend nor to be challenged. He thought he had been honoured by those who had chosen him to lecture but he also sensed he was a betrayer.

With apparent confidence he stood before his captive audience. From a majority he could expect support, but his eyes must not rest on members of the Christian union for they would be dismayed and alarmed as he delivered his oration. They would rename him Judas.

He sketched his family background. His father was a faithful preacher, known to many present, so he had been brought up in a religious atmosphere. Christianity, it had seemed to him, was the answer to the world's needs. He had read the Bible and prayed like a dutiful son, believing what he had been told, but now he had come to realise that the church had failed and if its teaching was not wrong it was inadequate. While it allowed the rich to remain rich, it allowed millions of peasants to remain desperately poor. The church's thinking was not in line with modern philosophy and while it was influenced by imperialism it was contrary to the welfare of China.

Those who had known Michael since his childhood, who had worshipped with him in church, were agonisingly perplexed. The climax of his lecture was frightening. He wished to accept the new leadership of China, to give himself without reserve to the thought of Mao Tse-Tung.

He resumed his place to find the crowd shouting a new slogan: "We greatly welcome the change in Michael and we are pleased with the progress he has made. We should make him our example and learn from him."

Not every speaker receives such encouragement! Other lectures followed but Michael's change of heart became the subject of intense discussion. His earlier refusal to compromise was widely known. Father, with sorrow, heard about the speech, then with mother prayed through the night.

Michael was acclaimed and a great future was prophesied. The Communists laughed at the mischief and offence his words would cause in the churches, and planned to publish them widely. "Your speech was really magnificent." There was hardly a derogatory comment, but he was not fooled by flattery and became depressed.

A few days earlier he had been playing basketball with a group of students when the ball hit him hard in the face pushing in a front tooth. He pushed it back again, not regarding the matter as serious, but after his speech he developed a high fever and his mouth became so uncomfortable that a doctor was summoned. He was instructed to leave the university and go home for three or four days, but that was the last place he wanted to go. When he arrived at our door, in obvious pain, father knew better than to criticise or scold. He was the eldest son, loved and respected for his sterling qualities. For months I had known that his faith was insecure, like a storm tossed boat without an anchorage, but seven years divided us and because of his success I almost idolised him.

For almost a week he remained at home nursing his swollen mouth, a conviction growing that this had been no ordinary accident, that God had allowed the ball to strike him with such devastating force. Tenderly fingering his face and the gum which would not stop bleeding, he talked to the God whose existence he had denied. He had to visit the hospital again but before leaving knelt and prayed: "If you really are God, creator of the universe, today as I go for my appointment with the doctor to remove the last bit of tooth let the bleeding stop." He stood up with little faith. The bravado, the triumph, the acclamation seemed a hundred years away. He had taken on God and the world and now he was floored by a small physical disability.

The doctor tilted back his head and removed the last fragment of tooth, stopping the hole with cotton wool. "Nasty," he said. "I want you to lie down for two hours and then to remove the cotton wool."

This will be the test, Michael thought, noting the instruction. In two hours I shall know whether my prayer has been answered. The minutes dragged. Again and again he checked the time. Eventually, he opened his mouth and removed the plug. There was no blood.

He almost wept. It had been bleeding for six days.

"Please God, forgive me for my unbelief, forgive me for my speech," he said tight with emotion. "Count me as one of your children. I do believe."

The exhaustion which had engulfed him disappeared. A fresh resolve gripped him. A new China? First there must be a new Michael. He had encountered God . . . a God on whom he would not again turn his back. At midnight he quietly went to our parents' room and found them both kneeling. He grasped mother's arm and whispered: "Pray that I may be forgiven."

No parents prayed more willingly, more thankfully.

The manuscript of his speech had been taken by the editor of the weekly newspaper. Michael, regretting every word, knew that if it appeared it would be reprinted in other periodicals as Communist propaganda. It would be quoted widely for years. Wherever he went it would follow him. Somehow he must stop publication but six days had elapsed. It was probably too late.

"God, what have I done, what can I do?"

Early on the Saturday morning he went to the editor's office where he was greeted warmly: they were glad to see him and hoped he was feeling better. The gap between his teeth was noticeable, but he assured them all was well. Everyone's still talking about your splendid speech, they told him.

"Regarding that," the editor turned to Michael, "the president had an emergency report which had to be used this week. Your speech has been put aside for the next issue. Sorry about that. Are there any changes you would like to make?"

Michael took the manuscript. God had heard his prayer before he made it. He glanced at the sheets then deliberately tore them into shreds. That will show whether or not I'm in earnest, he thought.

"Michael, are you mad? That was your speech."

"I regret making it. I should never, never have said what I did. I believe in God. I believe in His church. What I said was wrong. I want it to be known, to be known everywhere, that I am a Christian."

That evening at home we had soft noodles for supper

because Michael was unable to bite. He turned to me: "Mary, are you going to the Youth for Christ tonight? There is a meeting isn't there?"

"Yes," I said.

"May I come with you?" he asked.

"What? But Michael . . . yes, please do come." I played the piano at the rallies, but it was months since Michael attended, and I was quite overcome. My friends would be surprised for although they had been praying for him their faith was limited.

We walked there together. It took twenty minutes and we barely said a word, but there were strong feelings between us. I was proud to be seen with him, even prouder to be taking him to the rally.

After the preliminaries, before the sermon, there was an opportunity for testimonies. Michael stood up and with head bowed walked to the front of the church. He turned to the congregation. Those who knew of his university speech wondered what he was going to say, for he had declared his allegiance to the Party in a manner which left no doubt as to his future.

He spoke slowly and with dignity. He admitted his worldly ambitions, told of the pressures which had been upon him, of the invitation and preparation for the speech, and then went on to talk about his mouth which would not stop bleeding, and of his prayer. I watched and listened with brimming happiness as he told of his encounter with God.

"Last night," he said, "I came home at midnight to find my parents on their knees praying for me. Their prayers have been answered." There was a hush in the church as he turned to the chairman: "Sir, I have taken too long." "Please go on," he was told. "I have torn up the speech," he concluded. "God has given me another chance. I intend to live for Him."

Flushed he returned to his seat, an air of expectancy in the meeting. God could not be obliterated whatever the pressures. His firm stand brought wavering Christians back to the place of commitment and what he had said was printed and distributed among Christian students throughout China. There was a price. He was allowed to continue his studies but was dismissed from the positions of responsibility which he held in the university, and was mocked by former chums, "So a miracle happened to you!"

"Yes. To me it was a miracle. I will tell you more about it if you wish."

"You must be very careful," friends warned him, but he believed he must make a bold stand, or again be involved in compromise. Fanatical followers of the new regime showed their hatred in subtle ways, but openly were restrained in their persecution. It was early days and there was still talk about freedom, but with every month freedom became more of a memory, and soon it would not exist.

4

"YOUR father has been arrested."

It was the morning after he left home. Michael, to whom the information was imparted was unbelieving. The speaker was not reliable, but truth comes from odd sources.

"Surely not," he said. "It's a mistake, a rumour."

The informant shrugged his shoulders. Worse was to come. On January 4 a student who had been with Michael in high school and university drew him on one side.

"Michael, in your father's absence you are to face trial. In the park. It's fixed."

"How do you know?"

After slight hesitation the reply came.

"I've been chosen to accuse you."

"No."

"I have no option. The Party say I know you better than most, and they are aware our relationship has been a close one. I can't bear the thought of it." They were standing in the drawing office of the university engineering department. The scene was orderly and normal, not a setting for drama, but this information meant he might soon be in a labour camp. They had not forgotten the speech he tore up.

"Quick. You must depart from the city, go into hiding, vanish, and if you are caught please don't say we spoke."

"You've taken a great risk in speaking to me," Michael said. "Thank you."

At eleven that night he met two students whose judgement and discretion he trusted. Looking to see they were not being watched they left the university buildings and made for the sports field where they would not be overheard. He saw the dismay on their faces as he confided and sought their counsel. They were all maturer than their years, but this situation, threatening personal freedom, was too big. Friend was being turned against friend, preacher against congregation, patient against doctor, brother against brother.

"You'll not be a coward if you go," they told him. "And others may be involved if you stay. When there's a new climate return and continue your studies."

"I'll be back, if God wills."

The next morning was bright and chill. He went to the university as usual, wearing a new long gown, padded with cotton wool, which mother had made. He attended the lectures, although his mind wandered, and left the university at four, riding his cycle. He left his textbooks on the desk and other possessions behind and rode five miles to a small railway station. On the way he passed our home, giving it a loving last glance, but he did not stop. If he had entered the door his resolve might have gone. From a field used for public executions he heard gun fire, and when he arrived at the railway station he saw a public notice that twenty-six counter-revolutionaries had been shot that day. Had they ever tried to escape?

"I would like to give you my cycle. It's far from new, but it's yours if you want it." He had met a fellow Christian. The cycle, like thousands of others, was unlikely to be identified. The recipient gave him meat dumplings and purchased a ticket for him to Shanghai. He caught the last train that night.

China was in a major state of upheaval with numerous refugees and armed guards at all main line termini. Michael spotted the guards in Shanghai and as he drew near he saw them comparing passengers with photographs they held. A few were stopped but with barely a glance he was allowed to pass.

"Odd, but I'm not afraid," he told himself, acknowledging the peace in his heart. He now believed that father had been caught, but wanted to find news of him. Christian societies with international names once had their offices in Shanghai, but most were already closed, the missionaries having been sent home. The Salvation Army had been given notice to quit. A few China Inland Mission staff remained temporarily.

Michael, not knowing the Shanghai dialect, signalled a tricycle and wrote on a scrap of paper the address of the general assembly offices of the Chinese Church of Christ. The general secretary with his wide contacts throughout China might have news of father.

Michael believed that father had planned to go to Peking, but in fact he had made for Shanghai, where he had gone into hiding, thoroughly wretched, in a turmoil of conscience, convinced that he was a Jonah. He had avoided imprisonment, but he feverishly asked himself at what cost to his family? God was able to deliver, he had preached faithfully, but now he was parted from those trusted to his care. Separated from them when they needed his support and comfort. He had escaped trial by man to be tried by conscience.

He reflected on Bible characters who had stood forth in the name of God. There were no Communists then, but plenty of crossroads when men had to make a choice and sought Divine guidance and invariably found it. Had he been a Daniel in removing the photograph of Chairman Mao; a fool for God or just a fool?

"A wiser minister," he mused, "might have acted less precipitately. It's God's church. He can protect it. Was it by chance or destiny that I did what I did?"

He paced the small attic, his mind filled with dangerous thoughts, threw himself on the hard bed but unable to rest knelt by its side. He opened his Bible.

46

'If I ascend up into heaven
Thou art there.
If I make my bed in hell
Thou art there.
If I take the wings of the morning
And dwell in the uttermost parts of the sea,
Even there shall Thy hand lead me,
And Thy right hand shall hold me.'

There was no earthquake, or mighty wind or still small voice. He who had counselled others stood peering into the future, seeking answers which no textbook could supply, and he recalled what he had said to them. 'By faith Abraham ... went out, not knowing whither he went' (Hebrews 11: 8). He knew every Biblical phase of Abraham's life, how he had been uprooted by the voice of God, led from the settled place.

'Get thee out of thy country, and from thy kindred, and from thy father's house, unto a land that I will shew thee. And I will make of thee a great nation, and I will bless thee, and make thy name great ... and in thee shall all families of the earth be blessed' (Genesis 12: 1–3).

It was easy to go forth, he reasoned, but not to leave behind a wife, two sons and two daughters.

The treachery, the intrigues, the fateful decisions, pressed upon him. If I go back and die, he reasoned, at least my wife and family will know what has happened to me. Better they know than exist in suspense. I will go and consult the secretary at the assembly offices.

He was conscious of the tension as he crossed Shanghai. Most faces seemed blank or set in lines of anxiety for the city was filled with rumours. Unless God clearly guided him otherwise, he was going home. He knew the Biblical injunction: 'Be thou faithful unto death, and I will give thee a crown of life.' Other Chinese Christians had died for their faith in this and earlier decades, and there had been cruel massacres involving both Chinese and the missionaries cruelly known as foreign devils. It was no shame to die for one's faith or one's race. He had read of the fate of several million Jews in World War II; dying in gas chambers, in burning buildings, or ghettos where they failed to survive on a bowl of soup a day. To the sound of music they had marched into wash-houses for de-lousing to find there was no water but poison gas behind the hermetically sealed doors. Their offence was that they had been born Jews: at least he had chosen, voluntarily, gladly, to be a Christian.

He put the matter as objectively as he could before the church leader, telling of the request to borrow the church, the promises that had been made, and of his action when those promises were swept aside. The mass trial would have been an embarrassment to his fellow-ministers who had been instructed to set their faces against him. So he had left. Those were the dismal facts, but his strong inclination now was to return whatever the consequences.

The two men gazed hard at each other. The future for the church was becoming intolerable as the revolutionaries became openly hostile.

"On balance I think you should go back," the official said. "The alternative is to be hunted and harried. Maybe, I can't be dogmatic, your duty is with the people to whom you are pledged."

They prayed, remembering others who faced false accusations, who were being discredited. As they rose from their knees Michael entered the office.

"Son, how come you are here?" father demanded. "Have you come to fetch me? I am returning home immediately."

"No, father, you can't."

Both looked resolute.

"Why not?"

Michael explained his presence in Shanghai. Appearances were deceptive, for while much of life apparently continued near normal they were opposed by men of fanatical determination. Christians were being accused of espionage, sabotage, black marketeering – evidence was rigged. It was decided they should both stay temporarily in Shanghai.

Two weeks passed. Father had a plan and shared it with Michael. They would return home and Michael would hand him over to the authorities, saying he had discovered him in Shanghai. In this manner, father reasoned, Michael would go free. It was possibly a noble plan but God did not allow its fulfilment. Hindrance came through a student who arrived with newspapers from home. On four pages were serious accusations, in detail, against father.

"Christians will be dragged forward to give evidence against you," the student explained. "Wait awhile."

A second time they schemed to go back. Anyone staying in Shanghai for more than a few days had to register with the police. They had not done so, and dare not, and this was causing distress to others where they stayed. They must move. They planned to say farewell to a distant relative, but instead they received from her a severe lecture.

"Did you ever read in the Bible where God allowed people to return when He had called them out?" she demanded. "Is there a single example? I don't care where you go, but you cannot return. You must go on, forward, not back."

Three times God had hindered their return and they dare not consider it further. The relative gave her hard-earned savings to father and Michael. The gift came as a token of God's care and provision.

Michael and father separated. Father was given temporary sanctuary in a Christian household and Michael

49

moved in with a medical student. For five days as he studied the Bible seeking to know the next step the conviction came: "Go south." He shared it with father and a friend who offered to go and purchase tickets. "Where to?" he asked. "As far south as possible," Michael replied. He came back with tickets to Canton.

The train journey was of the stop, go, stop variety, taking two days and three nights. Every hour on the crowded train the passengers shouted slogans. One was: "You counter-revolutionaries, no matter where you try to escape, even to the end of the earth or sea the people's hand will reach you."

On the train passengers were jittery and some nerves showed signs of breaking. Each was suspicious of his neighbour. In any crowded carriage there might be an informer so little was said and sleep was almost impossible. Michael, his temples throbbing, went to the toilet to pray. There a fresh peace filled his heart and he returned to his seat with new purpose. He reminded father of the words of Jesus: 'My Father, which gave them me, is greater than all; and no man is able to pluck them out of my Father's hand' (John 10: 29). The Communists were powerful, no doubt about that, but God was greater. In His hand there was safety.

The slow, jolting journey ended at last and they arrived in Canton on January 24, spent and bruised. Their presence there seemed a miracle, although they knew nobody and did not know where to go. Not speaking Cantonese they wrote on a slip of paper *Christian church* and showed it to a tricycleman. They did not know to which church he would take them, but God would not make a miscalculation. At first it seemed He had. The pastor was unsympathetic. He had connections with the Communists which he was anxious to preserve and he advised them to return home. In his study as they talked father saw a photograph on the wall taken at an assembly in Shanghai. Father was in it. He pointed out to the pastor that they were there together. The pastor relented and gave permission for them to spend the night in his church but warned that if they did not leave the next day he would report their presence.

It was cold in the church, but as they were preparing to make their bed on the pews, there was a surprise visitor, who listened to their story and offered assistance.

"Tonight you will sleep here. Tomorrow I will be responsible and take you to another place."

The whole of the next day he was busy on their behalf. He contacted Christian students at the university. When one of the students heard Michael's name he remembered reading his speech and subsequent testimony. He wished to help and was introduced.

"Michael," he said, "there are a few thousand miles between my home city and yours, and we have never met, but it is as if I had known you for so long. God has brought you here at the correct time — not too early or too late. Tomorrow students travel to Hong Kong for the Chinese New Year. You and your father come with us. The condition of entry into Hong Kong at present is that you can speak Cantonese: tonight we teach you!"

It was a four hour journey by train to Hong Kong. On the way both father and Michael kept softly repeating the words which would get them through. Michael looked like other students, but not father. Their stomachs were churned at the prospect.

They queued with the students. Michael passed through, but when the officials spoke to father he did not understand a word, and those he had learned he forgot. The mental and physical strain of recent weeks were telling. His companions pleaded for him and Michael explained that this was his father, but to no avail.

"Go in peace, son," father said. "Do not worry about me. Acknowledge God all the days of your life. Go with my blessing. My life is in the hands of God."

Michael shook his head, unable to leave father, knowing the search that was being made for him. Without a pause he asked the guard to be allowed to re-enter China. It was a tense moment. The guard agreed.

The father of one of the students was the minister of a church on the border. He had worked there as a pastor for twenty years and his parishioners lived on both sides.

"Don't worry," his son said, staying with them, "I'll take you to Christians here who will get you over the border tonight." In a nearby house they changed into farmer's clothing. They had little money and were anxious if they could afford this service but no payment was asked, although those involved were at great risk.

After dark, their nerves screwed up, they left the house and walked for half an hour coming to a small river. Their companions carried father and Michael on their backs to avoid them getting wet. Soon they came to the border which divided China from British territory. There was a great wire fence, but the guides took them to a spot where it was broken. On the other side someone waited to meet them. In seconds they were through. A boy of not more than thirteen accompanied them for an hour until they arrived at a busy bus stop.

It was hard to believe they had emerged into a free world. Instinctively they breathed deeply. The crisp night air was the same. "I guess we should be very happy," father mused, "but we cannot be very happy while we are separated from our family."

"We are happy," Michael said, "but we are also sad."

The next day, their first in freedom, a sympathetic minister offered to take them to the cinema. They declined. It did not seem the way to celebrate their deliverance.

They were offered a temporary job as keepers of a large vegetable farm. They would be given food and allowed to stay in a small wooden hut overlooking the fields. For forty days they remained there seeing hardly anyone, each day praying and singing all the hymns they knew.

A Chinese doctor, living in Hong Kong, who was formerly a member of father's church, heard of his plight. She had been the midwife at the birth of some of us and now she offered them both a small house near Kowloon City. It was a necessary move for soon afterwards father became ill with dysentery and for a month Michael nursed him. Regular employment was difficult to obtain owing to the number of refugees from China so Michael did a variety of odd jobs. As news of father's presence spread he was given occasional preaching engagements but life remained precarious.

5

WITH alarm we waited at home for news of father's and Michael's whereabouts. Conflicting rumours reached us. It would have been easy to become hysterical, but mother asked God to give an assurance that all was well. It came to her through the ancient words of the Psalmist: 'For He shall give His angels charge over thee, to keep thee in all thy ways ... He shall call upon me, and I will answer: I will be with him in trouble; I will deliver him, and honour him. With long life will I satisfy him, and shew him my salvation.'

A staff member sent for me each day at school and asked: "Have you heard from your father?" I said nothing. "I will see you again tomorrow at ten." I was dismissed.

I was sixteen, not very brave, brilliant or cunning, but I was tempted to invent information which would stop him sending for me. At night, under the bedclothes, I would think of it, dreading the prospect of another day. As these sessions continued I became bewildered and insecure, but father, happily, was able to restrain himself from writing although the temptation was considerable.

At last Michael found a way of contact, involving little risk. He wrote to Canton, by arrangement with the students he had met, and from there a letter was sent to a relative who smuggled it to us.

For mother it was a glorious day when the first letter came announcing their safe arrival in Hong Kong, but she kept it from us for a while, it being vital that no one knew. One day she showed it to me with firm instructions that not a word must be said. I could still say, if necessary, that no letter had been received from father.

Our school, with its Christian foundation, was renamed, and so disassociated from religion. The premier, Chou-En-Lai, said he recognized the educational contribution of the churches, and it was of great value and merit, but that the Party would now provide better and larger schools and social services. He said this to Protestant leaders: it meant the end of Christian teaching in the classroom. God was struck off the curriculum even in schools with a religious foundation.

The church in China was being brought under a Government Board of Religion which embraced everything including Buddhism and Taoism. The Protestant section was to be controlled by the Three Self-Movement, the 'Three Selfs' being self-government, self-support and self-propagation. The alleged intention was to resist imperialism and western influence, but the deeper aim was to crush and control and not to allow genuine witness. Oddly, at first, some accepting the need for the Chinese church to be independent and self-supporting, did not see the real objective.

Christians began to compromise. We tried not to judge harshly, for the foundations were being hammered away, but there were incidents which grieved. At public gatherings father was criticised, and we were not surprised, but the wound was deep when a Bible woman who had laboured alongside him for several years made false accusations. She had been a fine woman, loyal, and one of the family; if she had refused to speak she would have been in trouble. Hostile to father or be classified hostile to the State.

Attendances in churches in the city slumped. "We can worship God at home," was commonly heard, and like the early church some met in private homes. No local churches had been closed, but in certain country districts there was open persecution and fearful stories reached us of believers being beaten and shot. Personal liberty was fast disappearing and soon all ministers would have to submit their sermons for approval by the local police: the routine being to take them by Friday night and to collect them on Saturday, edited. Experience revealed what it was wise to include or omit. There were themes which met with instant approval, ones which were heavily censored and a few which might lead to imprisonment. Never had sermon preparation been more demanding and faithful men of God asked themselves what the Apostles would have done.

In the cities like Shanghai there remained more freedom. China is so vast, bigger than the mind can comprehend, with communication often poor, that to generalise is impossible. In universities there was a strong Christian witness, and at 8 a.m. each Sunday I proudly joined about 100 young people in a small chapel. We carried our Bibles and hymnbooks openly, defiantly. There were several outstanding medical students, men and women, and their courage gave me strength. We pledged ourselves for Christ and His Kingdom, knowing we had a faith which was eternal and indestructible. We accepted that the church's record was not without blemish, but in Christ, our Saviour and example, we saw no fault. The structure might crumble, but Christ remained.

Our income from the church had ceased with father's departure. Church members would slip mother an envelope containing money, and Martin, always able to put his hand to anything, was able to cut stencils for evening schools. The piano teacher allowed me to take a few first grade pupils.

I pondered whether I should leave school to supplement the family income. There was a vacancy at the hospital for a trainee nurse and it would ease the burden at home. I talked it over with mother explaining that I would be happy to apply, but even happier if I could stay and graduate. It was perplexing for her. Father had wished for me to go to university and often talked of his hopes, but household expenses had to be met and prices had soared in the shops. Bravely, she reached her decision, and I shall always be grateful: "Even if we have nothing to eat you must continue your studies."

The larder was frequently nearly bare but we did eat. Mother missed father and Michael more than she confessed. An aunt came as often as she could, but she was criticised, putting herself in jeopardy, for aligning herself with the family of a counter-revolutionary. Father had left instructions that his books and notes should be burned, but it was a frightful task for they were so much part of him. He had thumbed and read them, and spent hours meditating on their contents, but his instructions were carried out. There were leisure hours in Hong Kong when he bitterly missed them.

Three times a year letters came from Michael, hinting that we should move further south, but until our schooling was finished this was not easy and we had absolutely no money to pay long-distance railway fares. We had never been financially well-off, but now the smallest coin had to be guarded. Clothes could not be replaced, yet others were also having it tough. "Give us this day our daily bread and, please God, may we soon again be a united family under one roof." I became quiet and suppressed. Worry lead to stomach trouble, adding to mother's anxieties.

Church members, particularly businessmen, were arrested and accused of being capitalists. "Who next?" the question was constantly asked, and mother stopped visiting friends fearing she might multiply their difficulties. Various young people close to us renounced their faith. Mother called us aside to warn us never to compromise.

"I pray that God will not allow you to deny your faith," she said. "You know what you have believed and I am

57

praying hard for you. God keep you faithful." She looked hard at Martin, Ruby and myself. "I would rather that you died than denied the faith."

I recalled her words when I was in medical school and was tempted to take the easy path. "I would rather that you died than denied the faith." Did she mean it? She did.

My piano teacher saw a musical career ahead for me, which meant that I must go to university. I was her senior student and she was proud of my progress, possibly because it owed so much to her painstaking effort. She was an assiduous teacher, who believed in making music as well as listening to it, and who knew how to handle the mischievous children who came to her for instruction. Her ambition was to make us all into musicians.

To enter university I had first to take the entrance examination held over three days simultaneously in all parts of China. Would-be entrants were invited to put down their first and second study choices. If they reached the required standard the government would decide whether these choices should be heeded or whether, for example, there was a greater need for engineers or doctors. Students had to take the examination in their own city. The one exception was music and those giving this as their first choice went to Peking or Shanghai. I was told it would be an honour for my school if I succeeded.

With four hundred other applicants I arrived in Shanghai for the music examination, but as I queued for the necessary documents an inner voice whispered, "medicine, medicine, medicine!" I had been influenced by medical students who spoke of the unique opportunities which a doctor has to witness to patients, especially to those dying. If public preaching ended, private, personal witness would become more vital than ever. From observation of father's ministry I knew the value of man talking to man and the doctor-patient relationship could be so close. For months I had studied and practised on the piano, sometimes finding delight and deliverance in music, at others disciplining myself to concentrate. Success would mean so much to my ardent teacher, to myself and to the family including father when he eventually heard.

The examiner at the oral examination was a professional composer and a Communist. I had described myself on the application form as a Christian and he started by asking, "Are you still a Christian, Miss Wang?"

"Yes, sir, I am."

"It is four years since Chairman Mao liberated us." He smiled indulgently. "It is a long time, but you have kept your old ideas. Perhaps you need re-education." Finally, he asked: "Miss Wang do you still wish to be a Christian?"

I wanted him to think I was tolerant, that I appreciated his lecture, and I did need him to give me good examination marks. My senses began to dull and I looked round in a dazed way. 'If any man will come after me,' Jesus said, 'let him take up his cross and follow me.'

"Sir," I said softly, "I intend to remain a Christian."

"Then, I'm sorry, but we have no room for you."

Nevertheless, I took all the other examinations and from 400 I was among those selected for final tests. I did my best, yet knowing the outcome. I owed it to my teacher. I was mortified, but elated that I had stood firm.

Four weeks later I scrambled for the newspaper when the results were published. A majority was forced to be disappointed for there were far too few places. It was a scorching, sticky day, and I looked through the long lists of names in tiny type. I was not among the successful music candidates. "Teacher, I am sorry. It was not your fault. It was not my knowledge, or my skill which failed, but my faith which was unacceptable."

I looked again. I had been accepted for the medical school. I was to train to be a doctor. The thought of dissecting bodies did not appeal, but clearly I saw the good hand of God. By taking the examination in Shanghai I was to attend a medical college there rather than at home. This was the start of a move south, a sizeable step in the direction of Hong Kong.

In Shanghai there was more freedom than in our city. Before the Communist take-over scores of foreign business houses had premises and staff there. There were miles of small shops and in the centre departmental stores. The best qualified teachers and college professors had studied overseas and had returned with a breadth of vision and a world view. In some respects it was not a typical Chinese city. It was now to be my home.

It was possible to get a letter to father telling him of my success. He preserved it and I quote a translation:

Dear Father,
How are you? How is your health? I often pray before God that He will keep you healthy and well. The result of the examination came out yesterday. I have been accepted by the first medical college of Shanghai to major in paediatrics. I thank God that He has guided His children even in this small detail. I believe firmly that whatever He has for me is all good. I pray that I may be faithful in my studies in order to glorify Him more. Everybody at home is well. I hope that when I am more settled here I will try to get mother to come to Shanghai. Let us trust all this in the Lord's hands. Ruby doesn't go to school and stays at home, but maybe this is good because wherever mother goes she needs somebody to take care of her. I am sure the Lord has a perfect will in all things. Apart from helping mother with housework she does some studies and practises piano playing, and

so has quite a full life. Martin graduates next year, then will be sent somewhere to work. After two years he might have another chance for further studies. Because this is his final year there is a great demand in his study and work and every time he writes to me it is at midnight. He is working very hard. I really thank the Lord for this. I remember so well that he used to upset you because he did not study. Now even when he recalls those days he gets fed up with himself. Aunt is not very well in health and is very tired because of her work. I have seen some of our relatives and your friends in Shanghai. Please do not worry about us. God will take care and continue to guide. Surely He will always open a way for us. I must stop here. May God bless you abundantly. Respectfully your daughter, Mary.

On my first day at the college as a medical student I was overcome by its vastness: its acres of ground, endless corridors, innumerable rooms and so many students. These were from several provinces, and that had educational value for those of us who had travelled little outside our own region. I was to share a dormitory with eleven girls, but I was the only Christian and later I learned the authorities were careful not to put two together. I met the girl who was sharing the upper bunk and she, like myself, was bewildered.

There were hundreds, literally hundreds of hungry, chattering students in the dining-room, each with a bowl, plate and cup, and a space in the cupboard to keep them after washing. I joined the impatient line which led to the chef, holding my plate and feeling shy and strange on my very own, and a long way from home, where my family could no longer shelter me. My dearest friends were beyond my reach. It flashed into my mind: 'Acknowledge Christ the first chance you have: the second chance will be tougher.' I wished it to be known that I was a Christian. What better way than by saying grace?

I sat down with my food and closed my eyes. "I thank you Lord for all these days and for leading me so far. At last I am here. I thank you for this food. I doubt if there are other Christians in the dining-room, but if there is one would you direct his or her eyes to look at me now." It was a long prayer for I continued: "Also, would you let the non-Christians see me so that there is no need for me to say that I am a believer. Amen."

As I opened my eyes I saw a girl walking towards me. I sensed she was a Christian. In some inexplicable way I knew before she said a word and she probably saw the change in my face.

"Dear sister in Christ, I welcome you," she smiled. "What is your name?"

"Mary." I was so happy. My voice shook. "Mary Wang."

"What is your major?" We were divided into paediatrics, medicine and surgery. I told her, but really I only wished to clasp her hand. She was my reward for confessing Christ. God in his graciousness had seen my aloneness and sent her to me. It was only the beginning. Eight young Christian men joined us, introducing themselves as members of the Christian Union. On this first day of a new term they had been scattered over the dining hall watching to find believers among the new students.

"You would not dare to assemble like this at home," I said, half afraid for them as they noisily gathered round. "Is it all right?"

They laughed, completely unafraid. "It isn't that bad yet in Shanghai," they said. I felt almost guilty at my good fortune as throughout the evening more Christians kept coming to greet me in my room. There were two thousand students in the college, one hundred of whom were Christians. Within days I had met them all.

In a small church, ten minutes walk away, we met almost every evening, sixty to seventy squashing in for testimony, Bible study and prayer. It was a simple building with no floor but God's earth. In Communist China, surrounded by millions who had been mastered by an almost bloodless conquest, we experienced the reality of a living God. Persecution had wrought a maturity and a depth in the students far beyond their years. No one could attend without being noticed: to enter the church was to proclaim one's testimony. The meetings were limited in duration as they were held between the evening meal and 8 p.m. when study recommenced. They continued until the end of my second year when the Communist grip tightened.

A girl in my room closely watched me kneel and pray before getting under my mosquito net at nights. Most of the girls in our dromitory came from Shanghai but she, like myself, was from another province and stayed in the college over weekends. After a month, one Saturday night as I read my Bible, books scattered all around, she said, "Mary, can I talk to you?"

"Of course."

She opened her suitcase and at the bottom, hidden away, uncovered a New Testament. She opened it and showed me the front inside page: 'From mother'.

"You are not a Christian," I said bluntly. "Why do you have a New Testament?"

I knew she was a member of the Communist Youth League. She had not prayed or joined us in the church.

"Look at this," she said.

Astonished, I read the letter she gave me which showed she belonged to a group of Christians called the Little Flock led by Watchman Nee. The letter was an introduction from an elder to the Little Flock in Shanghai.

"Do you know where the church is?" she asked.

"I have been there," I said, "but you . . . you are a

member of the Youth League. You have given no sign of being a Christian."

"I was afraid. You know how things are."

"But why didn't you tell me the first night you came here? You saw me pray and read the Bible. Why didn't you confide in me so that we could have helped each other?"

I may not have been as sympathetic as I should.

"I was afraid of the jeers, of the other girls. I am sorry. Would you take me to that church?"

We went together on Sunday and from then she openly acknowledged her faith in Christ, but it was so much harder for her than if she had declared herself on the first day. She was an intelligent girl. Now she was told that she must choose between Communism or Christ. It took courage to make the right choice and when her decision was known she was dismissed from the Youth League. I thanked God for her and we became close friends, giving support to each other.

Among the Little Flock I met a widow who invited me to her flat. She asked many questions about my family but at the beginning I replied cautiously for at that time we did not trust anyone, yet she proved to have such a natural love for me that I came to trust her and told her all that had happened. She listened attentively and I found being able to talk freely eased my burden. When I finished she questioned me about my mother and then made an undreamed of offer.

"Ask your mother to come and stay with me in Shanghai," she suggested. "Things are easier here."

"But that's too wonderful," I gasped. "Do you really mean it?"

"Yes, with your sister, Ruby."

My brother Martin had qualified as an architect and was beginning to provide financial help. I wrote to mother and told her to go to the local police for a pass. Explain that you are unwell and that I as a medical student could take more care of you if you were in Shanghai. Ruby had graduated from high school and while mother prayed on her knees Ruby went to the police, and secured permission for them both to join me in Shanghai. Within days they left their home and arrived at the widow's flat. To share her home with two other women was undoubtedly a magnificent gesture, enabling me to see them at weekends. Together we went to church and life seemed brighter, except for mother's continued ill-health and separation from father and Michael.

The China we knew was disappearing fast. Chairman Mao had said that he wished to eradicate the old Chinese culture, because it was inseparable from the old Chinese government and the old Chinese economic system. Under the new government there was to be a new culture. It had no place for God.

6

THOUSANDS of nationals were applying for exit visas from China and Michael urged mother and Ruby to join them in Hong Kong. He was now writing openly to our Shanghai address. I accompanied mother to the Shanghai police headquarters with a letter from Michael. I emphasised her health which was causing me anxiety and so hindering my medical studies. When the application was refused I waited two weeks, then re-applied, and kept doing so. At first I asked that Ruby also might go, but when I was told "Your sister is too young to leave China," I concentrated on mother. Reunion with father would improve her health.

In June 1954 mother was granted an exit visa. It was three and a half years since she had seen father and Michael. To leave Ruby, who had lived with her, was painful, and it was hard for Ruby to be left. Martin was working in the north and I was in medical college, but Ruby and mother had constantly been together. We all talked excitedly about the reunion in Hong Kong and did not hark on the possibility that we might not meet again. No one could predict the future political temperature.

After mother left, my college discovered the identity of father and obtained a detailed report on the family. I was called before the two college presidents, one a brilliant doctor, the other a high-ranking Communist who supervised political activity.

"We should very much like to help you," said the Communist.

"Yes, sir."

"You are doing well in your medical studies, but we

want you to be both progressive in your academic studies and in the development of the new China. You have seen what Communism is doing for China. You have read the writings of Chairman Mao, but with your background and a counter-revolutionary father there is much for you to learn."

I was to be detained at college during part of the summer vacation for systematic political studies. A room-mate, a convinced Communist, fifteen years older than myself, was assigned to me. She had been in the Party for years, and because of her contribution as a nurse to the Communist Army had been given the opportunity to study for a medical degree. We were to share a room for two weeks during which, from early morning until late at night, she would expound the benefits of the Chinese revolution. It was no holiday for her, but her success, and this was virtually taken for granted, would bring her great merit.

One final objective was to persuade me to renounce my father, refusing to have further contact with him. Self-criticism, which need not be wholly bad, was part of every-day life, and I was told to write my confession, everything from the age of eight onwards. My instructor could not have been more dedicated. There was no reserve in the way she gave herself to show me the error of my way and the benefits of the ideological struggle. I was concerned for the poor: so were the Communists. I was against corruption in the villages, the cities and the government: so were the revolutionaries. I wanted education for all, not simply for the favoured middle-class: this was now coming to pass. I did not approve of prostitution, black-marketeering, gang-sterism: had not the Communists done more to stamp out these aspects of life than Chiang Kai-shek?

After several days it was hard not to hate her fervour, although she was being no more than faithful to her con-victions. She was a warrior and words were her weapons.

She believed that Communism would conquer the world in her lifetime, and the belief was her inspiration. She was not driven, but drove herself.

We ate together, slept in the same room, and I was accompanied to the toilet. For twenty-four hours a day we were together, over and over repeating the philosophy which she unquestioningly accepted. Bible verses were used in an effort to convince me. Her patience was tried, for I was a bad pupil, and she must have found me unforgivably stubborn. We became irritated with each other until I could not keep myself from telling her bitterly: "But I thought our law stated that there was freedom of religion." "Yes, and freedom to oppose it," she retorted.

The crux was reached when the two weeks dragged to an end and I was still a convinced believer in Christianity. I refused to make the statement which would have brought her credit. There was a part of my nature which wished to please and conform, but I recalled the prayer I had made on the night of my public decision, whatever the cost, with God's help, to remain faithful to Christ.

Because of my non-cooperation I was informed that a mass meeting on July 16, 1955 would assess my case.

"You will face one thousand people," my companion warned. "If you are stubborn the crowd will tell you where you are wrong." As most of the college students were home on vacation it would be a meeting of local people.

'Persuasion corps' existed in every college and university, in industry for workers and management, in commercial offices and local communities. A few used terror but most a 'torrent of blandishments, promises, threats, mental torture and moral despair'. Suicides were commonplace, particularly among businessmen who were regarded as dangerous capitalists.

I was in distress, under pressure to cleanse my soul by confession, to reject all hostile thoughts about the State.

The hope was that I would be mentally liquidated, so that I would lose all love for my family and my old beliefs would be destroyed.

'The individual is nothing; all his personal beliefs are nothing; the Party is all, its acts are good and its pronouncements correct.' That was the daily proposition, but how could a Christian accept it? Jesus had shown the value of the individual and the importance of belief. I was inevitably hostile to the pronouncements of the Party.

My companion reminded me that if I did not respond to indoctrination there was reform through labour and this, or worse, I guessed, was the likely outcome of the mass meeting. Her constant presence and her own self-criticism was unbearable, and for her I was a heavy trial.

"I am sacrificing myself and my holiday for you," she said, and I felt base and mean. Companionship is a blessed thing, but too close proximity over prolonged periods can be a strain when there is no unity of spirit. "I want to get away from her," became a prayer. I understood why some confessed deeds they had not committed in the expectation that it would bring release. I should have been thankful that my interrogator was basically decent. Elsewhere businessmen had been tied to their desks or allowed to wear only underclothes, in freezing temperatures, for three days and nights. The manager of one company was locked in his office with interrogators who constantly demanded further confessions for seventeen days. Men and women were tortured, but the stress was normally not on violence, but on persuasion, re-education and thought reform.

Reports on the number killed in China during these years are unreliable, varying from tens of thousands to more than one million. One writer says ten millions. A large proportion were executed after summary trials at mass meetings, but a greater number were in labour camps where the work was unpaid and subject to strict control.

The inmates were known as 'enemies of the people' and were usually there for an indefinite time.

On the day before the mass meeting at which I was to be tried a small miracle happened. My companion left me *alone* in a ground floor room. She did not say where she was going but walked out through the door. It was nine o'clock, and a fine night, and I walked over to the open window. I could have climbed out but running away would have meant the end of my medical studies. Just to be alone was intoxicating. I relished every second.

I saw someone coming along the path which passed the window. It was a student, one of the Christians who greeted me on my arrival at the college, now in his final year in practice in the teaching hospital. The sight of an angel could not have been more welcome! He beckoned. I was frightened for him, but he was unafraid.

"Mary, I am praying for you," he whispered softly outside the window.

God had sent him I knew, and had sent my companion away, for the first time, so that he could say this to me, but I was so tense that I probably seemed ungrateful.

"Go away," I urged, thinking of his safety. "You will be in trouble if you speak to me."

I had not been allowed to communicate with anyone except my interrogator. He smiled. It was a smile that said everything: that the Christians in Shanghai, throughout China, and probably in the free world were caring and praying: that God had not forgotten one small Chinese girl. I wanted both to laugh and weep. He calmly walked away.

There was not a second to spare for as he disappeared my companion returned. She had been absent two minutes. I returned to my seat, pondering his perfectly timed visit, not knowing that one day he would tell me: "Mary, I was compelled by the Spirit. God sent me to walk past that window just then."

Almost at midnight, wondering what the 16th held, my companion said: "Let us go to sleep. The mass meeting is tomorrow. You will need to be alert."

Not only Protestants but Catholics also were facing the intensive propaganda aimed at destroying their faith. There had been about three million Catholics in China. Robert S. Elegant in *The Shape of Heaven* quotes a letter smuggled from a priest to Hong Kong: 'The Communists pretend not to force or impose their position on us; they insist, repeat, insist again and again; always around, in and out — and back to the same statement; wearing us out, breaking us down until, unable to hold out any longer, one is finally prepared to say, "Well, have it your own way!" But they won't accept it that way. What they want is for us to concede as if we had proposed it; as if we were finally convinced of what they have said and wished to surrender ourselves to their statements as if to our own self-imposed directive . . .'

Sleep was not going to come easily. Three or four months before an X-ray examination had revealed a chronic appendicitis, but for various reasons I had not been operated upon. There had been little trouble since. Before I finally closed my eyes I got up and knelt on my bunk to pray, thanking God for the unexpected encouragement, and requesting strength for the morrow. A little relaxed I fell asleep, but about 4 a.m. awakened with acute pain. It became so severe that I rolled about to find relief.

"God is this your hand of deliverance?" I gasped holding my side. I did not want to disturb my companion but she heard my smothered groans.

"What's wrong?" she asked suspiciously. I had eaten little food the previous day, but we had both put that down to my emotional state.

"I've the most terrible pain."

71

She had a thermometer with her and now fully awake took my temperature, reluctant to believe there could be anything wrong. She stared at it hard and then at me. The temperature was 103 which placed her in a dilemma, being a medical student.

"Stop pretending," she said harshly. "Nothing but nerves. Nerves and conscience, go to sleep." But she knew it was no act. I was sorry for her.

"My life is in your hands," I said, when I could get the words out between jabs of pain. "In your hands." At a deeper level the ultimate was in the hands of God; even the agony could not stifle that.

"Under no circumstances am I supposed to take you to the hospital," she said, "and that's the truth. Try to go back to sleep. The pain may have gone by morning."

She gave me some water. I drank a little.

"I'll try to sleep," I promised, wiping my brow, as she returned between the covers. "I will try."

An hour later, between five and five-thirty the pain became unbearable and she heard my distress. Her predicament was real as she had sufficient medical knowledge to know the risk she was taking by inertia, yet she was, I believe, under clear instruction.

I prodded her to action. I did not wish to be forceful, but I pointed my finger.

"My parents are not here. I am under twenty-one. If my appendix burst and anything happened to me you would bear the responsibility."

It was enough. We dragged on some clothes and she helped me to the hospital, a few minutes' walk. In emergency I was put on the couch and a doctor was summoned. When he arrived my companion warned: "She is on my list for today. Under no circumstances should she be detained in hospital."

The doctor was on my right and she was on my left. I

72

looked from one to the other. What power was in their hands, but only as God granted it. The doctor knew all about that list, and the possibility that someone would fake illness. I saw a nurse calmly standing by, in the tradition of her profession, but still in agony I closed my eyes and prayed.

The doctor, who was the registrar, hesitated only momentarily, then briskly instructed the nurse.

"Prepare her for the theatre," he said. "I'll be there straight away."

He looked into the eyes of my Communist instructor, and if she intended to object the words were not spoken. "You are a medical student. Remember the duty of a doctor is to save life."

She did not wish me to die and she was relieved that the decision had been taken out of her hands. By her warning she had amply covered herself if an inquiry followed. Wearily she went away, probably glad to be out of my presence. I was wheeled to the theatre where preparations were made.

I was not given a complete anaesthetic, but at 6 a.m. as the operation was about to begin two medical interns, both Christians, arrived to be with me. I was hardly in a fit state to ask questions, but later I learned that one had awakened with a compulsion to pray for me. It was the time when the doctor was making his decision whether to operate. Sensing all was not well, he dressed and made his way to emergency and saw my name in the admittance register.

To me God had clearly sent them; there could be no other satisfactory explanation for their presence.

> Behind the dim unknown,
> Standeth God within the Shadow
> Keeping watch above His own.

It was a difficult operation, with complications, and for two weeks I remained in hospital. I had missed the mass meeting on the 16th and I was allowed to go on the remainder of the vacation with no immediate threat hanging over me.

China was in a state of continued upheaval. A census revealed a population approaching 600 million, compared with 463 million in 1948. There were twice as many Chinese under fourteen as the total population of the Soviet Union; or more than the total population of Britain, Canada and America.

Mao Tse-tung was concerned that food queues did not grow shorter and that industrialisation was less rapid than planned. In July 1955 he ordered that collectivisation was to be speeded up. He complained about those 'tottering along like a woman with bound feet, always complaining that others are going too fast.' By 1957 more than half China's peasants would be working in collectives and all of them by 1960.

Reading the newspapers and listening to conversation, I knew I should be thankful for my deliverance. But I was slightly troubled: "God, am I not worthy to suffer for my faith?"

7

OUR early morning prayer meetings had to cease. They had been the subject of an inquiry. Each morning at six between twenty and twenty-five students had gathered to pray. In the winter months it had been dark and very cold on the flat roof of the School of Pharmacy, but no one complained about that. In a box in the straw were hidden thin cushions which saved our knees. We arrived silently, picked up a cushion and knelt in twos and threes. It was a place of refuge: 'For we have not a High Priest that cannot be touched with the feelings of our infirmities: but One that hath been in all points tempted like as we are, yet without sin. Let us therefore draw near with boldness unto the throne of grace, that we may receive mercy, and may find grace to help in time of need' (Hebrews 4: 15, 16). On other days it was a battlefield. David Brainerd, missionary to the Indians, said of such times: 'My joints were loosed; the sweat ran down my face and body as if it would dissolve.' It was then that with Christ in Gethsemane we prayed: 'Father, if thou be willing, remove this cup from Me: nevertheless not My will, but Thine be done' (Luke 22: 42).

The memory of these early morning intercessions remains as a fragrance with me. When a firm instruction was given that they must stop we discovered how good fellowship can be when two or three walk together along a quiet path or empty road. If it rained one could joyfully share an umbrella with another believer in order to have communion and prayer. As the rain came down our prayers ascended!

Unbelievably, there existed in Shanghai, a small

Christian bookshop, managed by Miss Helen Willis, a missionary, which was to remain open until April 1958. Miss Willis spoke beautiful Chinese. I was one of her customers, but she did not normally speak to anyone unless they spoke to her; this for their benefit as she was under observation. From her shop Sunday school material and devotional books went to distant parts of China. Her survival in Shanghai owed much to it being an international port: elsewhere her position would have been untenable.

When she was expelled she wrote a book *Through Encouragement of the Scriptures: Ten Years in Communist Shanghai* which was published in Hong Kong. She tells how the Communists feared and hated prayer. One charge against her was that she had supplied information used by the imperialists as prayer topics. She tells of a young man in the far west of China, an only son, who prayed for his widowed mother with an incurable disease in Shanghai. In prison he was told he would be released if he stopped praying; but he would not and his mother blessed him for it.

She recalls the pastor who was obliged to sell vegetables. He went round the homes of Christians, praying in each house, and so doing his pastoral work: the Christians saw that all his vegetables were sold by the end of the day. Many of his congregation were in prison, but a revival broke out in his mountain church and the number of believers increased from three hundred to three thousand. Miss Willis was able to get him Bibles and hymn books. As late as 1958 the church was holding special evangelistic meetings in the New Year, but the brave pastor refused to join the Three-Self movement and was imprisoned. His wife carried on, trying to care for the Christians, and her three children.

The courageous contribution of Helen Willis is remembered by those who like myself found her shop a spiritual treasure-house.

Ruby, my sister, was ill with extreme anaemia, and without the new drugs there seemed to be no cure. I applied again for permission for her to join the family in Hong Kong, but was told that if she had to die it should be in her own country as a demonstration of her patriotism.

Medical training in China normally takes seven years but an intensive course had been introduced which had shortened it to five. The first two years were pre-clinical, the third and fourth clinical, with the final year being spent as an intern. In the summer of 1956 I finished my third year.

There was a slight relaxation in controls and for a limited period passes were being granted for relatives to return from Hong Kong to the mainland to visit their families. Their safety was guaranteed. Mother wrote and suggested that we meet in Canton, but I doubted if I would be given travel documents for Ruby or myself. When I received her letter I told God: "To me this is impossible. By myself I dare not ask for a week's leave. You must confirm it if this is your will and plan."

I had a top bunk and with the moonlight coming through the window I was able to read my Bible after lights out. After I had prayed I reached for my Bible not disturbing those who slept. It opened at the Gospel of John and I read the words of Jesus: 'Let us rise and go'. I believed it was God's word for me. Next day I was given permission to take Ruby the two day journey to Canton.

It was a joyous reunion, and mother answered our numerous questions about father and Michael whom we had not seen for six years, but she kept her special news until the second day. "Michael will be joining us," she said. "He's on his way now."

"He mustn't, mother, it's too risky. They've got a file on him."

"We can't stop him, but he's very clever," mother said, "and will know how to answer if he's questioned. He will stay one night and then return."

Michael was now married and had a son. His wife considered his journey very risky, but God had given to him the words in Joshua 1: 9 — 'Have not I commanded thee? Be strong and of a good courage; be not afraid, neither be dismayed: for the Lord thy God is with thee whithersoever thou goest.'

We met him at the station, hardly speaking a word until we arrived back at our lodging. We made a meal with food mother had brought, then switched out the light ready for bed. Ruby, still unwell, went to sleep, but in the dark the three of us talked for hour after hour, sitting on the board beds.

Michael told how he and father had reached Hong Kong — twenty days later their escape apparently would have been impossible. In every sentence there was the undertone: 'Great is our God'. He wanted to convey that God had led us to this day and that we might yet be united as a family. Without Michael's help father would not have reached freedom. Hudson Taylor was said to have walked throughout his life 'knee-deep in miracles': that night we all believed in miracles.

"Whatever happens," Michael urged, "let Ruby stay in Canton. She should not return to Shanghai. Here she is near to freedom"

"She will be alone," I objected, "and who will provide for her?"

Michael was firm. "Tomorrow you will find a way. You may be able to get her into a school. Explain that her mother and father live in Hong Kong and that being in Canton may mean opportunities to meet."

Early in the morning he left, not wishing to take unnecessary risks, but mother remained for a few days. I accompanied Ruby to the local council office, approaching the official in genuine fear, but God gave me favour in his eyes. I spoke one sentence and he said: "You do speak beautifully." I was taken aback, but I was praying even as I thanked him for his compliment. Had not God given Joseph favour before men? I explained the purpose of our visit.

"Because of the way you speak I will do my best for you," this key official promised. I explained that if my sister was admitted as a pupil my mother could come in frequently from Hong Kong to visit her. "I am a medical student in Shanghai, and it will relieve my mind of the worry if she is a resident in a school here."

"I will help," he promised, my dialect still pleasing him. "Your sister will need to take an entrance examination for the high school and can sit for it in three days."

We swotted together. She passed and was accepted as a resident student. Before I left I told her: "Ruby, when your teacher asks say that your home is in Hong Kong. That's where you belong, with mother and father, not with me in Shanghai."

My brother, Martin, was in North Manchuria, one thousand miles from Shanghai, farther away than Hong Kong, but he seemed closer, for the free world was still beyond my comprehension. We were attached to each other; he sent financial assistance and I passed on information to him from our parents. Because mother's letters were opened before they reached me she had been guarded in her comment, but in conversation there had been no censorship. I was free to write to her, but outgoing letters were also scrutinised.

During my vacation in the beginning of 1957, Martin wrote that he was coming from Manchuria for a three week holiday. For two and a half years he had worked without a break. With fresh talk of freedom and reforms, and more food in the shops, it was easier to travel and everyone was taking advantage of this.

Martin and I travelled to Canton. Again mother and Michael came from Hong Kong, but father was unable to enter China. We spent another night sharing experiences. It was like a book, all these years of God's leading, a book to be read and re-read, so that we should never forget.

It was the end of term and Ruby's teacher asked her pupils who wanted permits for the holiday in Hong Kong. Ruby put up her hand. She was given one, so the four of us had a meal, went to the photographer's and the next morning Ruby left with Michael for Hong Kong. Martin and I took mother to the station and boarded the train with her for a few minutes. In China we rarely kiss, but she was in tears because even now she was leaving behind a son and daughter – impulsively we kissed.

"Mary, we have to depend on each other even more now," Martin said after a long silence as we travelled to Shanghai. He returned to Manchuria and I continued my medical studies.

In 1957 I completed the last term of my fourth year and earned my degree, but to be registered I had to complete the fifth year. To have passed the examinations was an intoxicating experience. They had been spread over May and June and I secured high marks, with other students having swotted until past midnight. It was not important that I excelled but to know, as a Christian, I had done my utmost.

The burning desire to be a doctor, to bring healing in the name of Christ although that name was barely whispered, had intensified since I came to the college. For me, on this earth, there was no greater vocation, nothing comparable. The vision was ever there. "Dr. Wang," they would say

On the eve of Father's escape, 1951. (*Back row, from left to right*)
Ruby, Martin, Michael, Mary. (*Front row*) Mother, Father, Aunt.

Father on the steps of the
church he built.

Martin played hymns after
school.

In the medical college grounds, 1956.

Mother in Hong Kong with Father, Michael, and his wife and son, 1957.

In Canton, 1957.

With Martin after the rest of the family has escaped to Hong Kong.

Below left: Michael says good-bye when I leave Hong Kong.

Below right: Pastor Wang with Gladys Aylward, 1951.

Congregation at the first service of the Chinese Church in London.

Nurses at the Chinese Church Centre.

Council of C.O.C.M. (*left to right*) Mr. S. K. Ng, Professor J. Fairbairn, Reverend F. A. J. Harding, Bishop Frank Houghton, Reverend George Scott, Pastor Stephen Wang, Reverend J. H. Hill, Mr. K. M. Quek.

Sunday service at the Y.M.C.A.

C.O.C.M. American Board. (*left to right*) Reverend J. Stearn, Dr. D. T. McIntosh, Dr. F. M. Pyke, Reverend C. Spicer, Mrs. F. M. Pyke, Dr. J. H. Pyke, Miss G. Davis, Reverend E. W. Hummer, Reverend R. Putnam, Mrs. D. T. McIntosh.

Dr. John Leighton Stuart,
former U.S. Ambassador
to China.

With Pastor Wang.

Baptismal candidates at Manchester Chinese Fellowship.
On Pastor Wang's right, Maylee Doa.

Ordination of Frank Cheung,
January 1971. Mr. Harry
Hughes, C.O.C.M. deputation
secretary on left.

With Father in Pastor Stephen
Wang's study.

Funeral of Pastor Stephen Wang, March 1971.

as I entered a sick room or hospital ward where I was needed. "Dr. Wang, you will know what to do!"

One year in a hospital and I would qualify. It had been a long haul, but not too long, for the prize was just ahead, or so it seemed in summer 1957. Father, separated for so long, would be proud, so would mother, and Ruby, and my brothers. With the examination over, our befogged brains cleared and joy flowed through our veins.

I did not know I would never be a registered doctor. Like Moses I was to view, but not to enter, to make the journey but not reach the goal. At least my goal. God had another. I did not guess.

Before commencing in the hospital I had two months holiday. It was unbelievable, for I had spent previous vacations in a factory, or on indoctrination courses, but now I had two months freedom, for relaxation, and the prospect was bliss. I would go back to my home city and be with the relatives and friends who remained.

It was four years since I had seen them. What had happened to father's church? Some of the congregation, with their love for children had inevitably spoiled us, and were almost as dear to me as my own family. They were part of the texture of my life, both light and shade, strength and weakness. I suddenly needed urgently to return: to walk the streets, to see my school, to be reunited. There is a pull about the earth where one is born.

I wrote to Hong Kong and told mother of my plan to go north, but her instant reply urged me instead to apply for a visa to visit Hong Kong. That year an agreement, which might not be repeated, had been reached between the Communists and the Hong Kong authority for students to visit relatives in Hong Kong without entry permits.

I sat down and re-read mother's letter. It was a very hot July day. The walls were hot and even the furniture, and everyone was perspiring. I always loved to hear from her. I studied her letters to see life through her eyes, to read between the lines, but on this occasion my immediate reaction was: "Mother you are hopeless! You have forgotten the life you lived in China. How dare I go and apply for a visa. Even to *ask* to go to Hong Kong would create suspicion."

There was a dossier on me and it was getting thick. My parentage, my faith, my record, nothing had been overlooked. I was afraid. It was possible this letter had been opened. Many were, but we were not invited to ask how or by whom. It was, we were told, to safeguard our minds from poison. How could anyone object?

I did not want to finish in a labour camp. I had friends who were already there, but I had other ways of serving Christ. I would put the letter in my drawer and forget it. I would not read it again as it upset me, but it was easier, far easier, to put it away than to forget it. From the moment of its arrival it filled my mind.

Of course I would enjoy a quick visit to my family in Hong Kong. Any daughter would. I was not lacking in affection: particularly I needed to see father again. An ache for him often welled up within me. I would like to have his hand on mine, to look into his face that so easily broke into laughter, to hear him. Memories from childhood flooded back as I recalled the last Christmas together.

"*Apply for a visa! Apply for a visa!*" No, I wanted to shout. I must not. Even for father I must not. It would be putting my career as a doctor at risk.

Throughout the miserable hot day I was in conflict. Mother did not understand the present situation in Shanghai. There were constant happenings which dictated caution. To be foolhardy, to step out of line, was not necessarily the will of God. There were saints who had suffered for their faith, while others had suffered for their indiscretion.

In the evening I stubbornly continued with my plan to visit my home city. No special documents were required. There were those there who would rejoice with me in my success in the examinations. A respect for education, for learning in any field, was rated higher than physical strength.

Finally, I prepared for bed, first kneeling to pray, but wherever God was it did not seem that I could contact Him. There was nothing but emptiness. I knocked and knocked again, but there was no reply, and it seemed there was no door.

"Lord, is there something between us that I cannot pray." Prayer, since a child, had been as natural, as instinctive, as breathing; the reality of God's presence a constant factor. For me, He rarely went on a journey. An absent God was not part of my experience.

Very clearly three Bible words came to my mind: 'Honour your parents.'

"But Lord, I do honour my parents. I have suffered for my father's sake and I have never forsaken them. Even now I am marked as their child and I am proud of it. I cannot do more than what I have done. If I have failed show me."

'Honour your parents.'

All day I had been refusing to listen to mother's letter. All day I had been arguing with it. The conflict had been real. My soul was scarred; but had mother been guided by God to write? had His hand held hers, His mind directed her thoughts?

Feminine obedience was part of Chinese life. An unmarried woman obeyed her father; a married woman obeyed her husband, and a widow obeyed her son. For centuries at least the first two had been upheld. Obedience was also a Christian virtue. Mother would not have written without prayer: that was a life principle. I could see her praying now. But sometimes praying mothers advised their children wrongly!

I was no longer a child. And, well, I did not have the nerve to go to the police for permission to visit Hong Kong. I knew what they thought of people who made such applications. If they gave me a visa it would be a miracle in view of my background. If not, there would be further evidence that I needed detention in a labour camp: dangerous inclinations to be re-orientated.

'Honour your parents.' I could not blot out the words. During that night my life, the past, the present and the future, seemed to be suspended. I did so want to be a doctor. Did mother know what she was asking?

"Do you mean, Lord, honour my parents at any cost?"

For me, that night, the answer was unmistakable and so, very frightened, I promised God that in the morning I would go to the police. I relied on Him for courage and He must take the responsibility! Sleep was even further than freedom that night.

With the dawn came fresh confidence, my terror passing with the night, and I resolutely, and with quietness, put myself into God's hand. I made an early start to the station where an official invited me to be seated. Soon began a three hour session.

"Why do you wish to go? Tell me the name of your relatives who are there? How do you write that? Now tell me your family history, from the beginning, missing nothing."

I had to remember the details for elsewhere the data was already filed and indexed and each statement would be cross-checked. I showed mother's letter and was given several forms to complete. At the end of the interrogation they retained the letter and promised to let me know their decision in writing.

As I left the police station my heart raced: "Mary, you stupid girl. Now it's done. You have committed yourself with your own hands."

One hundred yards down the street: "But, Lord, I do believe it is what you wanted me to do."

I had to throw it on God. With so many Christians in detention, my faith had dwindled to a tiny grain. For most there was no proper trial. Some were put on farms under strict supervision, others in factories far from home: professors were known to be on latrine duties, while students swept streets. Within the next decade thousands more would die for their allegiance to Christ.

A young doctor in our Christian fellowship had been sent away for witnessing about Christ. It was expressly forbidden, and he knew the risk. He had been in training two or three years when I arrived at college, and when I had my appendix removed he proved a true friend.

A patient was dying from cancer. He became very burdened for him and wanted to speak to him of Christ, but there was this strict regulation: if you had a faith in God on no account must you mention it to anyone. The doctor was in his final year and knew what it would mean if discovered breaking the rule. He gave what physical relief he could to the patient but withheld spiritual counsel. His own faith was so strong, that several times the words of salvation almost tumbled from his lips as he examined the needy man and sought to make him comfortable.

He paced the corridor. The inner voice was insistent: "Go and tell . . . go and tell him the Gospel before he dies. This patient is your responsibility. Your future is God's."

"I can't. I can't. It is not allowed." All the sounds and activity of a busy hospital were around him, but there was no escape. "Go and tell . . . go and tell."

He waited for an opportune moment. When the patient

was alone he asked: "Have you ever heard the name of Jesus?" The patient looked blank and the doctor told how Jesus Christ came to this world to be the Saviour of men, all men, everywhere. The patient, a seaman, said that it could not include him as he had led such a bad life. If the doctor knew . . . his conscience had given him no peace for years. The doctor explained that Christ died for sinful men, and in a few words sketched an outline of the crucifixion and the resurrection. "There is none other Name under heaven given among men whereby we must be saved," he urged.

"I want Jesus, I want forgiveness, but I am so insignificant that no one ever bothered to tell me about Him before," the seaman said in the last minutes of this life.

"You can ask Him to be your Saviour now," the doctor replied. He held the patient's hand and together they prayed.

As they did so a nurse peeped in to see how the patient progressed. She was surprised to find the doctor there. She had once professed Christ, but had given up her faith. She saw what was happening, knew the doctor was a Christian, and after the slightest hesitation made straight for the management offices. As a Communist there was no question about her duty. The doctor had deliberately broken the rule about religious instruction and she would share his guilt if she ignored the fact. Crisply, she told what she had seen. She was instructed to fetch the doctor.

"Now I am not afraid of death," the dying man told the doctor. "Now I will see God." He lingered for a few minutes, a new relationship established with God through Christ, then breathed his last. The doctor, a prayer of thankfulness in his heart, turned to the door. Outside the nurse waited. Immediately he knew.

"I've been sent to fetch you doctor. You are wanted by the office." He confirmed that the patient had died as he strode along the corridor. In the office the nurse repeated what she had seen and the doctor confirmed her statement. He had spoken of his faith: he knew it was against the rules: he could not heal the patient's cancer, but he had been anxious for the destiny of his soul.

"You are dismissed immediately from your duties."

He was directed to the building where those who broke the rules were housed. Later, a notice was issued stating that his final medical studies had been put back one year. During the year he would be adjusted in his counter-revolutionary thinking.

The incident served as a threat to every Christian medical student in the hospital. Outside there was more freedom. He had taught a Sunday school class in north Shanghai and in his absence I took it over. His family attended the church and his mother gave me clothes to give to the receptionist in the building where he was detained. Other Christians established a brief contact with him but after a few weeks he was sent away to the country.

His absence was a reminder that in a Communist régime there was no genuine freedom. Yet Christianity must be expressed; it springs up within the heart of a believer and has to find an outlet. An experience of Christ needs to be declared.

Two students, one a Christian, became firm friends, and inevitably began to discuss religious matters, always in private, behind closed doors or on walks when no one else was present. The unbeliever became an earnest seeker and expressed a desire to attend church. His enthusiasm bubbled and he began to speak openly of Christ. The outcome was that the student who had influenced him was sent away.

My reaction was uncharitable. "What have you done to my friend?" I wanted to ask him. "Why did you do this?" I had to fight what was almost a hatred for this seeker-after-God. I hope I successfully concealed my emotions from him.

The prisons were full, not of those who had committed robbery, murder, or bodily harm, but of men who admitted, "I was a reactionary. I spread rumours, I organised a group."

For most Chinese 1957 was a year of belt-tightening. Intellectuals, who were labelled 'rightists', were spotlighted. 'Serpents', said the *People's Daily*, 'can only be exterminated if they are brought out into the open.' Oddly, Helen Willis had a good year in her book room. Turnover in Christian books, posters, calendars and tracts was double that of 1956, but it was to be her last relaxed year. The following year her book records: 'We were not allowed to print the book on the existence of God. The sale of tracts and posters stopped. We had one order from the north for a hundred posters, but two days later an urgent letter came telling us to cancel the order ... Accusations were being brought against us, against some of our publications, against our connection with Wang Ming Tao, and especially against our dispensational chart. Many were afraid to come to the shop, afraid to borrow books.'

But your very presence in Shanghai, Miss Willis, was a reminder of the outside world, where Christians who worshipped freely, remembered their brethren in bonds.

8

I ALTERNATED from mood to mood, unable to concentrate, fearing, hoping, doubting, trusting, for the outcome of my application to visit Hong Kong.

On the Sunday I attended one of the assemblies where Watchman Nee used to preach, but it was impossible to worship there without remembering that he was in prison. I was not a member but went with a friend remaining there throughout the day with a congregation of courageous people. They did not pray like Jeremiah, 'Hast Thou utterly rejected Judah? hath Thy soul loathed Zion?' (Jeremiah 14: 19), but like Isaiah, 'Jehovah, even Jehovah, is my strength and song; and He is become my salvation' (Isaiah 12: 2). There was a morning service, holy communion in the afternoon, and a meeting for young people in the evening. It was refreshing.

As a school girl I had heard Watchman Nee preach when he visited a hall five minutes from our church. Although a renowned Bible teacher, he was a controversial figure, frowned upon by those who saw him attracting people from other churches. To a daughter, intensely loyal to her father, this did not seem good. His followers, I was told, almost physically compelled people in from the streets; though no doubt an exaggeration they were most active in open-air preaching and personal witness, distinctive in white cotton vests on which Bible texts were painted, giving away Gospel tracts. It was easy to be critical but when the crunch came they were clearly numbered among those whose faith held.

It was an Evangelistic service where I heard him, in his forties, well-built, an eloquent, convincing speaker.

His associates were often known as the Little Flock. It was a long, long sermon, even by Chinese standards, starting in Genesis and going through the Bible to Revelation, but his knowledge of the Scriptures was impressive, although I was too young fully to appreciate all he said.

In 1952 he was sentenced in Shanghai to fifteen years imprisonment, little knowing that he would not be released even when he had served those long years. In his book *Changed into His Likeness* there are addresses which he gave to Christians in Hardoon Road, Shanghai, in 1940. In a sermon on Jacob he said: "What God's hand does is right. Circumstances are His appointment for our good. They are calculated to undermine and weaken the specially strong point of our nature. It may not take Him as much as twenty years to do this, or it may take longer. Yet God knows what He is doing . . . 'Now for a little while, if need be, ye have been put to grief in manifold temptations, that the proof of your faith, being more precious than gold that perisheth, though it is proved by fire, might be found unto praise and glory at the revelation of Jesus Christ' (1 Peter 1, 6–7). There is nothing accidental in the life of the believer. It is all measured out to us. We may not welcome the discipline, but it is designed in the end to make us partakers of His holiness."

I first met his wife in Shanghai in my early days as a medical student. Later, my close friend was a neighbour of Mrs. Nee, their back doors facing each other. After her husband's arrest few dared to visit her, and to do so openly took great courage. Even in the assembly there was usually no open prayer for him, but silently Christians throughout all China prayed and have continued to do so. Through his books, splendidly edited by Dr. Angus Kinnear, his name has become familiar to thousands in the West who now added their intercessions. The Communists imprisoned his body, but his words, like those of the Apostle Paul, have reached the furthest corners of the earth.

I hesitated for some months before deciding to slip out from my friend's back door to see Mrs. Nee. Neighbours rarely talked to her. Eventually, I made the tiny journey. I greeted her and we prayed. I asked about her health, but we never mentioned her husband. A number of students paid similar calls: in the same way they had visited my mother at night, after father's escape, to avoid attention.

Unlike her husband, Mrs. Nee was of a quiet, reserved temperament, usually separated from the crowd, with considerable inner resources. She was also in my thoughts as I sat with members of the Little Flock that Sunday wondering about my future. Watchman Nee had been a successful businessman as well as a powerful preacher and Christian leader. His pharmaceutical factory had supplied antibiotics throughout China and almost all his employees were Christians, which made him a natural target. In 1952 most businessmen had been terrorised. 'Tiger hunts' had been organised 'to track down and destroy the vicious commercial tigers who prey upon the people's wealth.' There was no problem in multiplying charges against Watchman Nee — he was both Christian and businessman.

I was at home with these people with their love for Christ not extinguished by years of propaganda. Those who remained faithful no longer thought in denominational terms, but joyfully went wherever there was spiritual food, recognising each other as brethren in Christ. Barriers were down. Trifles which had separated, details over which we had debated and fought, administrative matters which had loomed large in previous years, were now of little consequence. Men of faith sought out each other, exercising caution in what they said, but instinctively knowing they were one.

There were leaders who had compromised, preachers

91

who read sermons about Chairman Mao. Helen Willis tells of a church in central China which issued its manifesto with the five 'goods' which all must follow — support the upright man, work hard, help everybody, study politics, be careful of hygiene. And the five 'no's' — no preaching outside the church, no house meetings, no faith-healing and casting out demons, no contempt for this world, no observance of Sunday or other church services to hinder work.

There was no compromise in Watchman Nee's assembly on the Sunday I worshipped there.

It was late when I returned to my room. Most other students had left for the holidays, but those who remained appeared to be asleep so I did not put on the light, silently climbing to my bunk. I felt rather than saw a piece of paper, and lifting it to the window, saw that it was an official document. I scrambled down and hurried to the bathroom to read it.

My visa had been granted and should be collected from the police station as soon as possible!

I had to convince myself that it was real. I read it again and again. It could not be someone playing a joke as I had told none of the girls of my application. I returned to my bunk but could not sleep. What would I do if they had made a mistake and now prevented me?

The next day the police official handed me the visa with a compressed smile. I tried to look assured, as if it were a normal occurrence, but my impulse was to clutch it and run, although I left with measured pace, then read the words anxiously.

It expired in two weeks, but this was later changed enabling me before departure to attend a five day students' conference at Watchman Nee's assembly. For some reason, I know not why, it seemed terribly important that I should.

I wanted to tell everyone that I was going to Hong Kong, to see father again, but I knew better for these were days when it was prudent for the lips to be sealed. To chatter was too great a luxury, for anywhere there might be unfriendly ears, and to confide in a friend could endanger him.

My secret leaked. A medical student, four years with me, approached and offered to queue for my ticket. But how did he know? He was an active Communist, a Youth League member, and he explained that he was also visiting Hong Kong and would travel with me. He would get *return* tickets for both of us. I had no objection, for I intended to return to complete my medical training, but who had told him about my visa? When I asked he merely said he had been told so I did not probe. He was not a stranger and he had a pleasant manner.

I attended the students' conference, but confided in no one there, although it was harder than I imagined to keep silent. We all had our individual fears about the coming months and these were reflected, if not mentioned, in our prayers and meditations. Those who follow Christ must take up their cross: equally, those who suffer with Him shall one day reign with Him.

I tidied up my living quarters and left my possessions in readiness for my return. Medics, like other students, travel light but there were several items which were of sentimental value. I was anticipating my year in a hospital, dealing with real people, and then achieving my ambition. I had told one trusted friend, a woman who loved mother, of my trip, and received her blessing. I took a last lingering look around my room, closed the door, and with the essentials I needed for the journey, went to the station.

The Communist medical student was waiting for me.

It was a two-day journey by rail from Shanghai to Hong

Kong and from what I saw and heard I knew the character of China was changing now more rapidly than at any period in her long history. In a few years Communism had taken authority not only in government offices, but in the minds of millions of peasants, students and businessmen. In 1921 Communist Party membership in China was about sixty: now it was numbered in millions, made up of cells of approximately twelve men and women. Not all of one mind, but all bound by a unifying purpose, with penalties that were horrifying.

I took out my Bible. Eyes covertly switched in my direction. I was self-conscious, and probably reddened, but it was not a new situation, and soon the passengers found other diversions and, almost forgotten, I read as the miles went by. 'Let not your heart be troubled; ye believe in God, believe also in Me.'

Some missionaries and preachers in China had undermined the authority of the Bible. So-called intellectuals, labelled Christian, had sown doubts about inspiration and reliability, but as I read there were no critical questions in my mind: I was not in a mood for argument but for communion with the Author.

From the Bible I turned to the hymn book which I had brought. There was a favourite hymn which I read and reread. Translated it means: 'God during the dark time you have been with me; I do not know what the future holds, but by faith I dare to trust no matter what may come; by faith I lean upon you and go forward.' It took the torment from my mind and gave peace in my heart. When it was dark I hummed it, possibly to the annoyance of some, but my companion confided that he liked the tune and asked me where I learned it. I showed him the words in the hymn book and explained, line by line, what they meant.

"My sister goes to church," he confided.

I questioned him and found I knew her, but had never

realised they were related. We talked for miles, getting to know something of each other, but both of us holding a part of ourselves in reserve. I opened my Bible to explain a point, but a passing Communist guard saw me, took a second glance, then came and ordered me to put it away. I obeyed. To have created a scene would have achieved nothing.

My companion proved an ally when we changed trains at several points on our long journey. It was very hot. There was no food available on the trains only at stations. I do not know whether the night was more tolerable than the sweating, endless days, but my heart leapt when, finally we reached Canton, the gateway to the free world.

There was frenzied activity and much excitement, but we wasted no time in travelling to the border where our papers were scrutinised. All was in order except that I had too much money! At least, more than I was allowed to take out of China and so, at the suggestion of the official, I posted the balance to Martin in the north. I was allowed to retain four dollars, enough to cross the border and board another train. It was my first experience of having to dispose of surplus money.

The last five miles seemed interminable but we arrived at last. As the train pulled in I saw Michael running alongside the carriage window. Father, whom I had not seen since the New Year's Day when he disappeared, was waiting. Love for him welled up. There was a lump in my throat and lots to say, but this was not the place, and he had my little nephew, whom I had never seen, with him. Tears were restrained with difficulty. The unbelievable had happened. We were reunited.

I introduced my Communist companion and mentioned his kindness, for his presence had made the journey less tedious. Michael offered a lift to his home, and said we would then go on to ours, which seemed a natural and right suggestion, but he refused. He asked us to take him to our home and said he would make his own way from there. Michael refused.

"We will go to your home first," he insisted courteously, not wishing to disclose our address. For him to have asked would have aroused suspicion for there was information that one did not readily offer.

We drove to his home, ignoring his protests. When Michael went with him to the door he discovered that his parents were not expecting him. His presence was a surprise, a pleasant one. "Why didn't you tell us you were coming? You could have sent a cable?"

Michael returned to the car, closed the door and turning the ignition key said: "Mary, you must thank the Lord. I believe that young man was sent by the Communists to find where you were staying, to report on your family, and to return you safely to Shanghai."

"That's how he got to know of my visit," I reluctantly agreed.

I should have felt safe, more secure than for years, but I was not. There was much traffic and I was tired. I assured my brother that I had not parted with the address. Among the large Chinese signs were ones in English, and although this was still the Orient there were more westerners than I had seen in years.

When we left the car to go indoors I sighed happily for at last the journey was complete. My kind sister-in-law, whom I met for the first time, had prepared a delicious meal and we all stayed the night in my brother's flat.

The date was August 3, 1957. We talked for hours exchanging experiences, and recalling God's goodness to us as a family. We felt like those who, thousands of years before, travelled with Moses from the land of Egypt.

"Let us trust God to get Martin out," father said. "We must never cease to pray for those who remain."

96

The swift-moving conversation switched back to father's own escape, the heaviness of his heart at being separated from his family and his church, and of his serious illness soon afterwards.

"But here I am, well, and still declaring God's word," he said with gratitude. "Thanks be to God."

I tried to explain Mao's recent slogan: 'Let a hundred flowers blossom. Let a hundred schools of thought contend.' He was saying, for a brief interlude, that Communism was not enough, that everybody should express their opinions openly, and nobody would be punished for it. "We shall see," Mao said, "which flowers are the best and which school of thought is best expressed, and we shall applaud the best blooms and the best thoughts . . . From now on, it isn't only 'Long Live the Communist Party' but also 'Long Live All the Parties!' We and the other parties must live in a prolonged period of peaceful co-existence and mutual guidance."

Father saw the statement as a trap. He was right. The freedom to criticise lasted about one hundred days, then critics were denounced and many lost their jobs. Mao had seen the underground opposition which had to be eliminated.

Father told how when he and Michael first arrived in Hong Kong, they had no employment, but a friend, formerly a doctor in our home city, had allowed them to build a small wooden house on her farm and there they stayed. It was a base from which to send down fresh roots. After twelve months he began to conduct worship for other refugees from China, and they provided some support. Later, he was invited to join the Christian and Missionary Alliance and for two years taught in their Bible School for the Blind which gave him access to books and theological papers. There followed his official appointment as pastor of the C.M.A. church for Chinese refugees, making his home in the refugee camp, where poverty was overwhelming. Houses were shoddily constructed from thin board which gave inadequate protection. Nothing was plentiful save fear and suspicion. The little wooden house, known as the parsonage, leaked when it rained heavily, but the door was always open, hospitality was freely dispensed. The authorities took little note of conditions in the camp which was united only in its opposition to Communism.

Yet to many the camp was a haven of which they had dreamed. Here, father explained, one dared to be oneself, to speak freely. There was no indoctrination, no terror, no slogans, no purges. Some had lost their families, others land or houses. Mao Tse-Tung had stated that eight hundred thousand people had been 'liquidated', but another estimate was nine million in the first five years of Communist control: no one really knew.

"Father, we must sleep if we are to make an early start," I urged. I had yet to meet mother and Ruby who were waiting at the parsonage for my arrival. After the journey and tension of recent weeks, I needed a long, unbroken sleep.

It was not to be, for next morning we stirred early and, after hurried refreshment, left for father's home. Later we learned that before nine o'clock there was a knock at the door. My sister-in-law opened it to the Communist student who had travelled with me from Shanghai. He had traced where I had spent the night, but my sister-in-law refused to say where I had gone. He returned later, unsuccessfully, to press Michael for the address.

"Welcome, welcome," mother said. "I've suffered agonies at the thought that you might not get here."

"How was the journey?" Ruby asked.

I told of the young man who had accompanied me. Glances were exchanged but little said. Confidence in people was running low.

My first reactions to Hong Kong were unfavourable. I did not like what I saw although I found it difficult to know why. The contrast was so great to Shanghai, where consumer goods were so scarce, and where many were frequently a little hungry. Here the shops were full but in Shanghai we had been allowed only three yards of cotton for a new garment. Tailors did a booming business in turning one's suit, coat or dress to the wrong side. Students, like myself, received slightly preferential treatment.

In Hong Kong, for those with money, there were no shortages, but the extremes between the haves and the have-nots was out of proportion to anything I had seen in China. The rich appeared to be daily getting more prosperous, but showed little concern for the poor. I reacted against the extravagance and waste. It seemed unforgivable, as un-Christ-like as Communism. I had to get used to Hong Kong currency, to making a choice in the shops — surprisingly difficult — and to a freedom which was bewildering after a tightly controlled regime. Here was freedom, but freedom for what? I was dismayed, when I knew I should be jubilant. I saw corruption amongst those who loudly condemned the revolutionary Mao Tse-Tung. Had I, after all, been brain-washed?

Rumours started to spread. How did Pastor Wang get his daughter out? Some who had tried without success to bring relatives from China, considered I must be a Communist to have been given a visa. Father, knowing a small group of fanatical refugees might harm me, feared for my safety in the camp. Also, because my travelling companion from Shanghai was endeavouring to trace me I went to stay with an English missionary doctor, Stuart Harverson. He had a small private sanatorium for thirty to forty patients where I was able to assist.

I was in a disturbed emotional state. I was under pressure from mother and others to remain in Hong Kong, but although I loved my family I did not wish to stay, but to return to Shanghai. Outside China there would be no recognition of my medical qualification: my years of study would be wasted when the prize was almost within my grasp. I had a return ticket to China and had every intention of using it, but the pressures became so considerable I feared I was going mad.

Father, knowing how passionately I wanted to be a doctor, and yet wanting to find a compromise that would please mother, although without any savings himself, offered to raise the money so that I could start fresh training outside China.

He took me to the university to see a professor friend to discuss the possibility of my entering its medical school. I was told I would have to start my training again: father was told the cost. Examinations I had passed in China were not recognised. I knew virtually no English, and many of the textbooks I had studied in Shanghai were in Russian. Before I could commence medical school, stage one, I would have to return to high school, and the thought of becoming a schoolgirl a second time was unbearable.

I tried to face reality but I could not think clearly. I wanted to do what was right and decent, I wanted to be true to God, to my parents and to myself, and constantly I prayed. I became bad-tempered and feared I was about to break up completely. Never had I been so tangled.

The choice: A doctor in China, with no freedom to talk of Christ, under tight Communist control . . . or a refugee in Hong Kong, with freedom, the comfort of my family, and no status.

After three weeks I confirmed to mother that I was definitely going back, returning before my visa expired. I would take up the hospital appointment which would form my final year's training as a doctor. God would not have permitted me to go to medical school, I reasoned, if He had not wished me to qualify. I had a duty. I was returning to it.

With as much restraint as she could muster she warned me that if I returned I might never be free to leave China again. It was a fair assumption. I might be saying farewell to my family for ever. How did that register in my reckoning?

"Mother, it is natural for you to want your children with you. Good mothers always do. I hate the thought of separation even for a few months, but you know my heart's wish. I have studied to be a doctor — what could I do if I remained in Hong Kong? There's no future for me here."

Father viewed the matter more objectively but finally he came down in support of mother. He offered to write to a medical school in Taiwan to see if I could complete my training there. Those last seven days before the visa expired were a nightmare. I was under no illusions about life in Communist China although I could not foresee the horrors of the next decade. For a doctor, I imagined, life would be hard but tolerable, although I knew of professional people doing menial tasks in labour camps. Further, I loved China: whatever its faults it was my country, my home, my inheritance.

I had a terrible dream. In the dream, it was a nightmare, I had returned to China, but had nowhere to sit or stand in its millions of acres. There was no place for me to put down my feet and rest. It was so vivid that I awoke trembling and with relief found that I was in Hong Kong. From that moment I changed my mind. I knew that I must not return to China to live under a compulsive, godless regime.

The deadline came and I made no attempt to pack my bags, and when it had passed I knew a measure of peace. Before the dream I refused to hearken to my parents, to accept their most reasoned arguments, but after it I needed no persuasion although my heart was heavy.

Father gave both moral and spiritual support. "Mary," he said, "it was the Lord who opened the door for you to come out. Of that I am sure. Bide His time. He has a future for you. One day you will see how the pieces fit into shape. Whether you are to be a doctor time will reveal, but one day you will understand why you had to go to medical college."

The dream proved the turning point, but my pride, my reluctance to lose my identity, to part with my ambition, remained.

I assisted Dr. Harverson with his sanatorium, and the patients called me Dr. Wang, wanting to show their respect, and for some months it acted as a balm. His wife, not sparing herself, gave me English lessons. Always, of course, I was under the supervision of this dedicated doctor, but gradually I came to accept that in spite of my training I was unqualified. The title I accepted was false and was dropped.

My patients, I found, had spiritual as well as bodily needs, and the opportunities to give spiritual counsel for which I had ached in China were plentiful, but I did not always grasp them. Such is the way of the human heart. There were days when I almost doubted God — how could He be a God of love? — but out of the blackness came a stronger faith, and I accepted what appeared a bleak and uncertain future.

The Communist student, who had been my companion, returned to Shanghai alone. He left a letter with Michael protesting strongly. The Communists had fed me, given me the opportunity to study, and generally indulged me, and this was my way of saying thanks. There was truth in what he said. I summoned courage to write to the college to ask for a record of my medical training. I received a swift reply. It instructed me to return to Shanghai without delay and threatened that if I did not do so I would be expelled from the college and my records would be destroyed.

I did not mind being expelled. It hurt more to know that all traces of my being a student and of my examination marks would disappear. I did not know the prayer of St. Augustine, but he expressed my cry: 'Let my soul take refuge from the crowding turmoil of worldly thoughts beneath the shadow of Thy wings; let my heart, this sea of restless waves, find peace in Thee, O God.'

9

My decision to stay in Hong Kong meant separation from the Christians and the Chinese church which survived on the mainland. Inevitably, my thoughts constantly returned to those with whom I had worshipped at home and in Shanghai. No one could predict the future of any individual, events occurred too swiftly, but I knew the Chinese church was one that would not die, although for a bitter period its voice might be silenced. The church is not buildings, which may be confiscated, or clergy, who may be imprisoned, but the church is the Body of Christ, made up of those who believe that Jesus is Lord. The New Testament did not refer to the saints who met in a particular building, however consecrated it might be, but to the saints in Rome or Ephesus. The structure might vanish, but not the saints.

I am told that Dr. Chia Yu Ming has died. I recall him preaching in a small room, crowded to the doors, in an old house in Shanghai. There was no formal order of service and the doctor appeared only minutes before he was due to preach. But what preaching! As a young man he had planned to go to America to study theology, when brilliant students were advised to go overseas to complete their training. He went on board ship and was waiting for its departure when God said to him, "You must not go. There is no need for you to go to America to study theology." It was as clear to him as if he had heard an audible voice. He picked up his luggage, went down the gangway, and returned home. There were exclamations from those who had bid him farewell, but he had received his instruction, and there was no question in his mind. A notable scholar, Chia

Yu Ming was the author of many theological books and he was ultimately given a doctorate by an American university — without ever stepping off Chinese soil!

What has happened to Mr. Wang Ming Tao, pastor of the biggest church in Peking? His influence throughout China was even greater than that of Watchman Nee. He refused association with the Three Self Patriotic Movement which had given an undertaking that the Chinese church would support the Communist party in return for certain freedoms. Until 1954 he was constantly proclaiming, in the spoken and written word, the evils of Communism. A fearless man, because of his strong convictions he had been in trouble all his life. He was dismissed from a school where he taught after conducting a baptismal service for new Christians by immersing them in a river when the temperature was near freezing. In the 1920's he was jobless for three years and the larder was often nearly bare, but he took his fill of spiritual food, using the days in Bible study, until he knew more of the Scriptures than most doctors of theology. He attended school with Pastor Stephen Wang, of the Chinese Overseas Christian Mission, and they had been good friends. Wang Ming Tao travelled through China preaching and lecturing and great crowds, often one thousand or more, gathered to hear him. Students found him stimulating, and in the medical college fellowship we avidly read his quarterly publication *Spiritual Food*, almost the last devotional magazine to survive. He would not, could not, compromise on any Biblical truth, and it was inevitable that he would be arrested. For months he carried a small parcel, in readiness, containing Bible, pyjamas, toothbrush.

In 1955 the police went to his home. "We have come to arrest you," they said. "I was expecting you, and am almost ready, but please let me change my clothes," he replied.

He was accused of being a counter-revolutionary. Those who had been associated with him had to renounce him or risk imprisonment. To possess a copy of any of his publications was dangerous: these had been carefully preserved by hundreds of pastors and Bible students, but the majority were now burned. I had often read his work.

After a year or so he was released. It was said that after brain-washing he had signed a confession: certainly those who met him had no doubt he had been subject to considerable mental strain. Some declared he was temporarily unbalanced, but his conscience gave him no peace. "I have denied the Lord," he told his family. "I am like Peter." He prepared a fresh statement retracting anything he had said in prison and asked the Communists to publish it. Instead, he was rearrested, remaining in prison until 1968, when at the age of sixty-eight, he was moved to a labour camp in north Shansi. We do not know more.

When I left Shanghai I had not heard of the Chinese church in London, or its minister, Pastor Stephen Wang, although he was later to play a decisive part in my life, but in Shanghai I had met his daughter, Sung Ling, a teacher at the seminary where Dr. Chia was president. She had graduated from Yen Ching university and then studied at the theological seminary in Shanghai. After graduation, she remained to teach New Testament Greek.

The authorities, I remember, tried very hard to persuade all such tutors to return to secular professions if they had one: if not they were to learn a skilled trade such as carpentry. The new China could no longer countenance them living from the contributions or labours of others. Oddly, the Bible was quoted: tutors, like preachers, were reminded that the Apostle Paul was a tent-maker.

Christian teachers and professors did not refuse to engage in manual labour, but they did refuse to compromise their faith. Tutors at the theological seminary made a firm stand for Christ and in 1958 news leaked to Hong Kong that they had all been imprisoned in a labour camp in north-west China. Sung Ling received a ten-year sentence. After one year she developed tuberculosis of the spine, but no treatment was available, and she continued working fourteen hours a day. Her health deteriorated and her spine became permanently deformed.

From London Pastor Wang endeavoured to send her medicine, but it was refused. A letter came from her: "Pray for us. We are in Gethsemane and on the way to Calvary."

Before her imprisonment Pastor Wang had written urging her to escape from Hong Kong. Her carefully worded reply said: "The seed of the Gospel is sown by God's people and it needs to be watered. Now we have to water it by life and blood. You are my father and I should listen to you, but it is to be ordained by the Lord Himself otherwise."

Sorrowful as he was to receive such news, the letter nevertheless later proved a great strength to her father.

Martin was still in China, when, in January 1958, mother had a slight stroke which affected one side of her face. My parents had prayed continually that he might be with us. I had heard father through the thin partition which divided our rooms talking to God about Martin. "I want my son. God, You have brought us out one by one, surely You will complete the family. Friends say how lucky I am to have three of my four children, but I want Martin with us, too, Lord." I could not sleep and joined him in prayer.

Days later mother had the slight stroke which provided the reason for Martin's visit. It would be two months before she recovered, but nothing could be a better tonic than his reappearance.

I offered to write to my brother asking him to apply for a

visa to visit her. The family agreed that I should do so and the letter was sent. Martin was himself sick in bed when it arrived, but he dressed and went straight to the police where, because of mother's sickness, he was immediately granted a permit. Within twenty-four hours he was on his way, leaving his watch with a senior colleague who did not possess one. Martin had a good work record and his family connections had never been itemised at the local police station. No one suspected that he would not return.

He travelled first to our home city where we had lived as children to greet those who remained. It was a brisk, purposeful visit, and a week later he reached Canton, from where he telephoned Michael in Hong Kong. My sister-in-law answered the 'phone and told him he would need a permit to enter Hong Kong.

Application was made but the Hong Kong government said no. It was unbelievable. In Hong Kong the responsible department could not believe that the Communists would allow a young man of Martin's ability to leave without an ulterior motive. For three days he was in Canton, on our doorstep, but unable to reach us, and shortly his permit would expire.

Michael approached Dr. Harverson and begged his aid. The doctor was holding a clinic that morning but, realising the urgency, he sent all the patients home telling them to return in the afternoon. He accompanied Michael to the permit office and offered to act as guarantor for Martin. If Martin stayed he would give him employment: if there was the slightest trouble he would see that he left Hong Kong. The necessary documentation was provided.

Dr. Harverson, now with the Worldwide Evangelisation Crusade in Viet Nam, had been a true friend.

Michael crossed to Canton, went to the hotel where Martin was staying and found his brother asleep. He hastily dressed and together they hurried to the local police station to cancel his registration. This formality over they went to the check point to freedom where it was found that Martin had lost the entry permit. They both searched their pockets frantically but it was not there.

"We had it in the police station. Let's go back," Martin suggested. "I must have dropped it there."

Halfway back they found it on the ground. When they returned to the check point the official looked at the date. It expired that day. Tomorrow it would have been impossible to leave.

All the family were now in Hong Kong. It was hard to contain our joy as each told of God's leading in the years of separation.

Father explained how useful his knowledge of Braille had been. He had learned this years before when he had been a trustee of a school for the blind. After his illness in Hong Kong, the Christian and Missionary Alliance, an American society, which had done a notable work in China, were looking for a man who could speak Mandarin and read and write Braille. He was appointed and found himself living with thirty men, ex-soldiers who had lost their sight fighting in the nationalist army. For two years he taught them Braille using the Bible as a textbook, plus music, also lecturing in the society's Bible school. After two years, in 1953, he became pastor of the Christian and Missionary Alliance church for refugees where he was to remain until 1968. During his ministry father built two churches: one at home, at the start of his ministry: the second in Hong Kong, for the refugees just before he retired.

After it was decided that I would settle in Hong Kong I entered the Christian and Missionary Alliance seminary for a Bachelor of Theology course. I was mindful of father's challenge, when I was a girl, that one of his children might continue his ministry. Normally, the degree course took four years but because of my previous studies a concession was made and mine was fixed over three years. I did some teaching to cover the cost of food and accommodation, and during the vacations worked in the sanatorium where Sister Annie Skau, a Norwegian missionary, was the matron, and my very dear friends Grace Liu and Mary Wong, were her assistants. Whether a radiographer, a laboratory technician, or in the pharmacy, I adored this break from the classroom, knowing again I was back in my sphere.

I took journalism as an extra subject, and the lecturer who knew my background, encouraged me to think of a future career in Chinese Christian literature. It was an attractive proposition, although I knew I would continue to miss hospital life. Pride was never far away. I told myself, in baser moments, that if I could not be a doctor then I would not be a nurse. The persistent, inner storm raged, as I swotted for my thesis, but God was re-moulding my stubborn character.

Music was a consolation. When my nerves were over-charged it gave release. I was given the privilege of teaching the piano to other students, for the President Dr. William C. Newbern was a gifted musician as well as a fine theologian and always emphasised that none of the seventy young men and women would graduate without being a modest hymn-playing pianist.

I was surrounded by those who showed understanding and love. If most young people go through a time of adaptation, when they are liable to bring their parents to despair, this was mine. I was urged to think of missionary service, but I was looking to God for the next move, fearful of a misplaced step.

In early 1961, Pastor Stephen Wang came from London to Hong Kong seeking news of his daughter, whom I have mentioned, and his wife. His wife had been in prison, but was now released. On her return home she had written to him: "The grace of the Lord Jesus is sufficient for me. Please pray for members of the church. Give thanksgiving and praise to God."

My father and Pastor Wang had been at college together and they met in Hong Kong by chance, if that is the word, at the hotel where my father was visiting another evangelist. It was in March that father introduced Pastor Wang to me as Uncle Stephen, and since that hour I was proud to be regarded as his niece. His arrival in Hong Kong was not publicised. Mr. Michael Stewart, the British Foreign Secretary was there, and representations had been made to him about Mrs. Wang and Sung Ling to see if the Chinese government could be approached on their behalf.

Pastor Wang was standing outside a restaurant when a young man passed by, backwards and forwards. "Excuse me, sir, but what is your name?" he asked.

He was a former student of the Pastor. He took him into the restaurant, which was really closed, giving him a splendid meal, but afterwards Pastor Wang saw the announcement of his arrival in the Hong Kong press. The former student had told a journalist, who had also known the Pastor as a college lecturer, so the visit was no longer secret.

I first heard Pastor Wang preach when he spoke at morning chapel in my seminary. I was the pianist that morning. His text, from Jeremiah 18, was about the potter and the clay. 'And when the vessel that he made of clay was marred in the hand of the potter: he made it again another vessel, as seemed good to the potter to make it. Then the word of the Lord came to me, saying, O house of Israel, cannot I do with you as this potter? saith the Lord. Behold, as the clay is in the potter's hand, so are ye in mine hand.' He told how he had been called out of China for another ministry, still to the Chinese, but in far away London.

Afterwards he stayed to lunch. It was my turn to be on the top table where he sat, but to give more space to the guest I moved elsewhere, so had no chance of conversation. Later, after father's 'accidental' meeting, I, with other members of the family, was introduced. Father asked about life in London and Pastor Wang spoke of my going to nurse there. Apart from the fare there was nothing to pay, the training for state registered nurses being free. If I wished to go he would do his utmost for me. I explained that I was thinking of a literature ministry and he did not discourage me, but later spoke of the need for someone to assist in a work among the hundreds of Chinese nurses in Britain, preferably with their kind of background. There was a Chinese missionfield in London, with absolute freedom of speech and liberty, and he was looking for someone like me!

He volunteered, when he returned to London, to find a hospital where I could do nurse's training, giving my off-duty hours to the Chinese church. My English was slowly improving, but the thought of study in that language was not pleasant, so I said I would think about it while studying for my degree finals, and consult my tutor in journalism. I felt an obligation to him, for I believed he was counting on me. Before I talked to him I prayed: "God control this. If he is very upset may that throw light on what You want."

When I told him about the Chinese church in London, a branch of the Chinese Overseas Christian Mission, he listened sympathetically. "Well, Mary, maybe this is the path for you. You have had medical training and God can use this . . . But I do hope you will do some writing."

Pastor Wang left Hong Kong at the end of March. He had arrived believing that he might return to London with his wife, and possibly his daughter, but this was not to be and he was now compelled to accept that he might never see them again in this world. His disappointment was overwhelming, but he said little. Forever surrounded by people, there would always be a lonely place in his heart.

I was not quite willing for what he had suggested, but some weeks later he wrote to me. He had talked with the matron of King Edward Memorial Hospital, Ealing, in the suburbs of London, and she had provisionally offered a place for training! What reliance she placed on the Pastor's recommendation. The Pastor suggested I wrote to the matron, so half-reluctantly, half-eagerly, I composed a letter on the lines he suggested, and with only the faintest notion of what life in England would be like I committed myself. My application met with a quick response. A handwritten letter from the matron suggested that I join the school for trainee nurses commencing in July, but because I was graduating in June it had to be the next intake in October.

I had not resided in Hong Kong for five years and so was still a stateless person. When I applied to the emigration office they explained that I would have to wait twelve months to complete five years.

"All right," I said hastily, walking away.

"Come back," the clerk shouted. "Leave it with me to see what I can do."

Three weeks later I was given the necessary documents, but still needed the equivalent of five hundred U.S. dollars for the air fare, having no savings. Father promised assistance, but I refused believing that if God wanted me in London it would not be at his expense.

At the Hong Kong convention for missionaries, a sort of Keswick get-together, I met an American missionary who had stood by me during my studies, with prayer, and small gifts often in an hour of genuine need, thus strengthening my faith.

"Mary, I have heard you are making plans for Britain," she said.

"Do you think I am right?" I needed reassurance.

"Come and have tea with me," she said. "Then we can talk."

She questioned me about my plans over a cup of tea and asked about the fare. "Who's going to pay it, Mary?"

"God will provide," I faltered.

The next day she telephoned, asking me to go to her office. When I arrived she explained that B.O.A.C. had told her there was a cheap air fare for students. "God is wonderful," she went on. "A businessman came yesterday, after you left, and gave me five hundred dollars to give to a student in need. I knew at once it was for you. If you take this cheque to B.O.A.C. they will give you your ticket."

Tears came into my eyes. This Presbyterian missionary herself was not rich, except in faith, but God had trusted her as a channel for my need. As I took the cheque all my doubts vanished about whether I should go to London. I had been clinging to my medical training like a dead body; it had been a heavy, tiresome weight which had held me down. Now I let it go. I was like Pilgrim when the burden rolled away. I was grateful for my training, but it belonged to the past, and a light was shining on a future path. Our accomplishments can hinder our progress as much as our failures.

Busy days followed, with packing and farewells. In a short time I had accumulated all sorts of odds and ends which had to be jettisoned. Saying goodbye to my family was not easy after the long years of separation, but we all tried to be brave.

I had never been in an aeroplane before, but after the take-off I settled down for the long journey across the world, and arrived in London on September 22, 1961. Pastor Wang was in Germany but I was met at the airport by a representative of the British Council and given a lift in a van to King Edward Memorial Hospital. I gazed hard through the window, but as we did not go through central London I did not see any of the sights I had heard about — the Houses of Parliament, Westminster Abbey, Buckingham Palace. Outside the main hospital entrance I met the matron, who took my typewriter and called a porter to take my luggage. She saw I was apprehensive.

"Don't be frightened, Mary," she said, gently. "You'll be well looked after, and you can come to me whenever you have a problem."

She summoned a Chinese nurse who spoke Cantonese, and after a wash I had my first English meal. The fish, chips and peas were appetising, but I could not manage the peas with a fork, and no one used chopsticks. I was shy, a bit homesick and a little lost and hurriedly retreated to my room to write home. Although because of my English, my training would not be easy, I sensed I was in the right place.

West Ealing, I found, was a quiet residential district. During the ten days before my training began I went out in the mornings for walks, admiring the lovely rose blooms in the gardens. People who kept their gardens so beautiful could not be fearsome I reasoned. One day an elderly couple greeted me "Good morning," they said brightly. I wished the ground would open up so that I would disappear for I doubted my ability to converse. "Are you a new nurse at the hospital?" they asked. I slowly explained that I had just come from Hong Kong, but when I left them I felt that now I really belonged in London. I was on speaking terms with two of its citizens.

My first weekend was with an English family. A third year nurse at the hospital took me to the Christian Alliance Club in London, from where we travelled by underground rail to Cockfosters. At the Oak Hill theological college the students were on vacation, but we occupied a dormitory and were entertained in the home of the Principal, the

Reverend Maurice Wood. Mr. Wood was away, but his wife, Margaret, made us doubly welcome, and on the Sunday we attended Christ Church, Cockfosters.

Pastor Wang was soon back from Germany. I went to meet him at the House of Rest, a Christian guest house, in St. John's Wood, where he lived. About eight young people were in his room cooking a meal but although they were Chinese they were all speaking English. Even here I could not conceal my language problem. When they left for a choir practice I settled down with Pastor to tell him the news from Asia.

10

THE Chinese church in London was the pivot of my English life. Free evenings and weekends when perhaps I should have been visiting St. Paul's Cathedral, built by Sir Christopher Wren, Dr. Samuel Johnson's house, or standing outside 10 Downing Street, the residence of Britain's prime minister, I scurried to the church or to the House of Rest. It is easy to be lonely among London's millions, but I was not.

Pastor Stephen Wang, founder and director of the Chinese Overseas Christian Mission, of which the Chinese church is a thriving part, came to England in 1948, studied at Cheshunt College, Cambridge, and later lectured in Birmingham. At home he had been Principal of the Methodist College in north China and, on completion of his studies in England, he planned to accept an academic appointment in America where his family would join him. The temporary separation was accepted by his family: none could foresee what would happen.

The youngest of his five children was five years old when he left China. Each was to excel scholastically, two qualifying as doctors, but he was never to see them again. For years there has been no word. During his stay in Hong Kong the total outcome of his endeavour to secure their release was a telegram allegedly from his wife: "Blood pressure too high. Cannot travel." Whether she sent it he did not know.

In 1948 the American Ambassador in China offered to keep a watchful eye on the welfare of his family during his stay overseas. "If there is an emergency," he told the Ambassador, "I leave you to make arrangements for the evacuation of my family." Twelve months later the Ambassador recommended that Mrs. Wang and her family, and his own wife, should leave China, but they refused. When the American Embassy in Nanking closed, the Embassy staff returned to the States, but Mrs. Wang, still optimistic, remained in the country of her birth.

In England Pastor Wang, with the William Paton Lectureship at the Selly Oak Colleges, Birmingham, was teaching students from ten countries. It was an interim appointment before taking up permanent residence in America with his family. Meanwhile there were opportunities for travel in Europe. No matter where he went he met Chinese families and because of their spiritual need he challenged the missionary societies, whose work in the Far East had been curtailed, to do something for them. He spoke to missionary executives and wrote letters:

"I thank you for sending missionaries to China. My country is indebted, but may I remind you that on your own doorstep there are many Chinese who are spiritually neglected. I beg you to appoint ex-China missionaries to minister to them."

In 1949, on a visit to the Continent, he spent five sleepless nights considering his own future. He consulted mature friends and wrote to his family. Should he return to China, where the Communists would limit his ministry, or should he take up a teaching appointment in America and settle there with his family? There was a third uncomfortable possibility. Should he launch out alone, with no guaranteed support, and accept the challenge of the Chinese who were migrating in swelling numbers to Europe? All agreed, including his family in China, that at least for the present he should not return home.

His appeal to the missionary societies found its way on to the agendas of responsible committees, and was debated in one large conference, but the societies stated they were already fully committed elsewhere. In their view the hour was not ripe to branch out in this way.

Career-minded friends urged him to go to America, but increasingly he believed the finger of God was pointing to a London-based ministry to the Chinese. It meant throwing his academic career to the winds. It was a crucial point in his whole life, but could he deliberately turn his back on security?

Last century another Methodist, William Booth, had stood at a similar crossroads. His wife Catherine, who was to become the mother of the Salvation Army, wrote to her anxious parents: "God sets before us our duty and then demands its performance, trusting solely in Him for consequences. If He had promised beforehand to give Abraham his son back again, where had been that illustrious display of faith and love which has served to encourage and cheer God's people in all ages? If we could always *see* our way, we should not have to walk by faith, but by sight . . . I don't believe in any religion apart from doing the will of God. Faith is the uniting link between it and the soul, but if we don't do the will of our Father it will then be broken . . . I cannot believe that we ought to wait until God guarantees us as much salary as we now receive. I think we ought to do His will and trust Him to send us the supply of our need."

During Christmas, 1950, when my father was removing Chairman Mao's portrait from our church, Stephen Wang in London was taking the first steps in obedience to God's call. On Christmas Eve, at the House of Rest, and again on New Year's Eve, there was a meeting for prayer and discussion about the Chinese in Europe. On Sunday, January 7, 1951, the Chinese Church in London was born in the home of Mr. and Mrs. K. T. Fan. Thirteen attended the first service, including nine Chinese, but numbers grew until the lounge of the Fan's home was inadequate, and in July 1951, meetings commenced in London's Central Y.M.C.A.

Pastor Wang recalled the start of the church in a 1952 issue of *World Dominion*. "Though I felt disquiet within myself about the Chinese yet I had no intention of doing anything for them personally . . . Two years ago, while I was preparing to return to China, God called me for this work. I wrestled with Him because I knew that it would be very difficult to commence a new work in a strange land without any financial backing, that it would mean a long separation from my family in China, and that I had no message to preach. The Holy Spirit guided me to the potter's house for a period of time, where He convinced me of the richness of our heavenly Father, reminded me of how the early disciples left all behind, and revealed to me the message to preach 'Jesus Christ, and Him crucified', from whom we receive our wonderful salvation, that we sinners can become saints and the dear children of God. There I surrendered myself and offered myself as a piece of clay into God's hand to be moulded according to his wish. He moulded me from a teacher into an Evangelist. It was a glorious emancipation from old bondages and responsibilities, and a wonderful joy in a new career as an ambassador of Christ.

"After my experience in the potter's house I came out to make contacts with Chinese in London and Liverpool. Things are always difficult at the beginning, and my work was by no means an exception. However, after a few months of wondering, through the wonderful guidance of God I met Mr. Edward Low, a Christian medical student, and later I made acquaintance with Mr. K. T. Fan, of the School of Oriental Studies."

At the first anniversary of the church on January 6, 1952, 130 were present. In the week Bible studies, prayer meetings and a social meeting on Saturdays were held. Pastor Wang paid eighteen visits to Liverpool during the first two years, each visit lasting for a week or so visiting the various Chinese laundries and seamen's restaurants and in door-to-door visitation.

He had a burden for the Chinese throughout Europe, in Africa, and other parts, where there were no missionaries concerned for them. "In order to fulfil this obligation," he wrote, "our Chinese Overseas Mission has been formed to recruit men and send them to the various places where the need is greatest. The chief aim of the society is to carry a positive Evangelism to the Chinese outside China, and to bring them a knowledge of the full Gospel of salvation through our Lord Jesus Christ. The work is based upon the simple preaching of the Bible as the inspired Word of God. In the second place, it is desired to help the Chinese Christians to establish their own church in accordance with the principle of self-support, self-management and self-government."

It was a surprise to Pastor Wang on arrival in Britain to find that his own countrymen were out of touch with Christian influence. He soon found the same about his own countrymen on the Continent. At that time the Chinese were still running more laundries than restaurants. "Those in the laundries work very hard, they go to bed late and rise early. They labour so hard in order to obtain means of existence that their outlook upon life becomes materialistic. Intellectual and spiritual interests are neglected under the immediate pressure of securing daily necessities. 'Man does not live by bread alone, but by every word that proceedeth out of the mouth of God.' They need the Gospel, they need the Christian outlook on life, they need Christ the Saviour."

From the beginning there was an emphasis on prayer. "Prayer is needed for preparation in the propagation of the

Gospel," Pastor wrote. "Prayer is our co-operation with God for carrying out His plan of salvation. 'The harvest is plenteous but the labourers are few.' Some have said that labourers are not only those who preach the Gospel, but those who labour in intercession. More prayer more result, much prayer much result, no prayer no result. This is true regarding work amongst the Chinese in England. It is difficult to find a Christian among the Chinese, owing to the lack of Christian work among them. This is due to the lack of prayer for them. China itself is often prayed for, but if you want to save the souls of the Chinese on your doorstep you must pray for them, and pray earnestly and constantly."

In the first twenty months three residential conferences were held. A memorable one was at Frinton-on-Sea, about fifty miles from London, in the summer of 1951. A letter recalls how 'the Eternal Spirit of God broke us down and deeply humbled us before the cross. One and another cried out from the depths of his being as, in a measure, we realised the awfulness of the clash between God and sin upon Calvary. An overwhelming sense of His holiness bore down upon our spirits . . . words failed . . . tears fell, as the Holy Spirit made intercession for us with groanings which cannot be uttered. It ended with a triumphant note of praise and thanksgiving to God for his unspeakable gift.' Some verses by Anna R. Sheng expressed the burden of the conference:

> The needs of the Chinese Christians
> Are known in the realms above;
> And God in infinite mercy
> Still loves in infinite love.

The dispersion of the Chinese population was only beginning, but already, the conference was told, the figures were challenging. Philippines 9,295,511; British Isles 8,000; South America 21,443; Japan 93,715; North America 216,383; Europe excluding Britain 22,397; India 14,964; Middle East 8,148; Australia 35,248.

In 1953-4 Pastor Wang visited various European countries. He met Chinese in business in Stockholm, and found four Chinese restaurants in Copenhagen. He visited Dutch universities in Amsterdam, Leiden and Delft. In Holland there were about 800 Chinese students from Indonesia, and the first of 150 Chinese restaurants.

No one knew him when he went to Paris in 1953, but near the Chinese quarter he found a Protestant church. Its location was ideal for his purpose, so he traced the minister.

"Will you kindly lend me your church for three weeks?" he asked.

"But who are you?" the minister reasonably demanded. "I do not know you. Is there someone who could introduce you?"

Pastor Wang could not think of anyone who might know both him and the minister. He took out his wallet to get his card and as he did so a photograph fell out. The photograph taken in Cambridge, included some French students.

"Do you know anyone in this photo?" Pastor asked.

"Why, this is my cousin," the minister exclaimed.

"And this is me," Pastor Wang said pointing to himself.

He had the use of the church and no charge was made.

In Cardiff, South Wales, with its extensive dock area, and in Liverpool, considerably rebuilt after bomb damage, there were special evangelistic efforts.

In 1955 a team of six organised intensive visitation of Chinese families in Liverpool, culminating in public meetings which were attended by between 150 and 200 people.

There were both discouragements and conversions. The team met an old Chinese laundryman who had been bedridden for nine years since the closing of his business. A few days earlier he asked for his old trunk to be brought to him. In it he found a small booklet with the Lord's Prayer printed on the cover. He read it and believed that God would soon answer his need for inner peace. When he was visited both he and his wife wept. They attended the evening meeting the following day, the old man in a borrowed wheelchair, and two days later he became a Christian.

In London, the Reverend John Stott, Rector of All Souls' church, at the top of prosperous Regent Street, made available a room for weekly Bible study. Evangelical leaders were taking note of this Chinese ministry in their midst. The weeknight meeting was subsequently transferred to the premises of the Evangelical Library.

In summer, 1955, a team of five visited Paris. Four were making their first visit to France, but there had been much planning and briefing in advance. Efforts were made to seek invitations to evening meals in the homes of Chinese residents so neighbours could be invited in. A start was made at the Embassy. After the meal a short Bible study was held with each present being given a Gospel. On several evenings they met in the home of a businessman who had been a student of Pastor Wang's in China.

Visits were made to a cement factory outside Paris which had sixty Chinese employees. There were happy hours with Mr. Jolson Fang, a convert from Pastor Wang's earlier visit who was in hospital recovering from a lung operation. In a sanatorium for tuberculosis patients there were nine Chinese. Two had been there for five years and had been seldom visited. The visitors were able to take food and fruit prepared by the owner of a Chinese restaurant who saw that none of the team went hungry.

A pattern of Evangelism had been established and was

repeated in 1956 in two evangelistic campaigns in London, three in Cardiff, two in Holland and one in Paris.

The Chinese Overseas Christian Mission, which had owed much initially to the Reverend F. A. J. Harding, a banker in London, being introduced to Pastor Wang by Miss Lily Armitt, an ex-China missionary, now needed premises of its own. While every need was met between 1950 and 1960 there had never been a surplus to put aside for building, and often the accounts barely balanced. In 1960 Bishop Frank Houghton, of the Overseas Missionary Fellowship, a China veteran, was elected chairman of the C.O.C.M. Drawing from the experience of Hudson Taylor, he gave a stirring word based on Jehovah-jireh – 'God will provide'.

More than one hundred years ago, he reminded his audience, Hudson Taylor then a young missionary of twenty-five, living at Ningpo, China, chose two watchwords for his life, and had them written in Chinese as a pair of scrolls. Later they became the watchwords of the China Inland Mission (now O.M.F.) which he founded in 1865. The first watchword was 'Ebenezer', which literally means 'The stone of help', set up by Samuel to commemorate a victory over the Philistines. 'Hitherto', Samuel said, 'hath the Lord helped us' (1 Samuel 7: 12). For the future the watchword was 'Jehovah-jireh' meaning 'God will provide' (Genesis 22: 14). Abraham had just seen God providing for him in a spectacular way, and he was sure that He would continue to do so: Hudson Taylor had similar faith.

Bishop Houghton went on to say that when the young missionary founded C.I.M. he opened an account in the bank with ten pounds, for that was all the money he had. He had not the backing of any wealthy people, or of any denomination, but he believed that God would provide both money and workers in answer to prayer. Over the years hundreds of missionaries went forth, relying on God alone, and not on any human organisation.

It was the word C.O.C.M. needed. In November, 1960, special intercession was made for premises. On November 4, after three hours of prayer, the sum of £1,500 was promised, not from a large group of wealthy people but primarily from students whose means were limited but who were moved by a spirit of supplication and sacrifice. Through the post came gifts to be sold including a jade ring, a gold pendant and a pearl brooch. The American Board of the Mission, set up in 1959, found 120 friends to give support.

In 1960 the European Council of the Chinese Overseas Christian Mission came into being with Bishop Houghton as chairman and the Reverend George Scott, of the O.M.F., as vice-chairman. The vision given to Pastor Wang in 1950, had grown, as more of the world became his parish. He knew that not only in the west but throughout south-east Asia the Chinese could best be evangelised by the Chinese.

Two members of the London church returned to Malaya for their summer vacation in 1961 and held evangelistic services in the New Villages. Peloong Chin, then a medical student, on return wrote:

"We walked across the ditches and entered the crowded houses steeped in darkness and idolatry. The children were lively though unkempt and ravaged by indescribable diseases. Their elders eyed us suspiciously as we passed. They had not forgotten the time when they were uprooted from their homes which were by the fringes of the jungle and transported to New Villages living under a state of curfew and behind perimeter fences. Now the 'emergency' is over, but many still live in fear not of the terrorists but of evil spirits.

"As I walked with the other members of my team, the sorrows and fears of these people touched my heart very deeply. I know that only the Lord Jesus can answer all their longings and fill their lives with a new hope. But how are they to know and trust this Jesus of whom they have never heard? Who is going to tell *our own people* of His love and power to save?"

A stranger in London, I found myself in this Chinese mission, witnessing to my own people. At every service there were newcomers who were welcomed and invited to stand. (Today stewards give each a folder explaining that this is a London home for those from overseas. On the back is a statement of faith. On a visitor's card they write their name and address and the reason they are in London. They are given a small red silk ribbon which they pin on their coat, and after the service are invited to an evening meal. The young people take it in turns to cook for between sixty and seventy: not a lavish menu, often rice and noodles; and this is followed by short talks, discussion or films. A lot of effort, but we talk rather of the results.)

The emphasis in the church was on winning souls and developing Christian maturity. One of our members wrote in *The Reaper* before my arrival: "We live in an age of miracles. Week by week we are eye witnesses to the transforming power of the Lord Jesus in saving our friends. We see that God hath delivered them from the power of darkness and hath translated them into the Kingdom of His dear Son. With what joy we report that since the beginning of this year over one hundred souls have been brought from darkness to light. Blessed be God. The Gospel has been preached not only in the church but at all our gatherings and the Lord has blessed consistent witnessing for Him at flat fellowships, Malayan Christian fellowship and Hong Kong House fellowship . . . Each of us has been called to be His ambassador. In our colleges, hostels and 'digs' we have constant opportunities for 'offering the Lord Jesus' to our friends. Even in the past month we all rejoiced when two 'seven months old babes in Christ' led two Chinese patients in hospital to the Lord. What are the incentives that made these two converts 'fishers of men'? The answer is 'the love of Christ constraineth us'. In the words of one of our members, 'Because Christ died to save me from my sins and has given me His more abundant life, I want to tell the world of my wonderful Saviour'."

II

In Autumn, 1966, I went to America for my first visit. With Pastor Wang I was to tell about the Chinese Overseas Christian Mission. I wondered how I would be received by the American people, for Chinese Communists had made no secret of the fact that America was the sworn and implacable enemy. I need not have worried. Everywhere there was enormous interest in the Chinese Revolution and in the welfare of China's millions. The churches which had provided so much support for missions were eager for news and from countless citizens I received extraordinary kindness.

Americans may hate Communism and fear its foreign policy, but Americans do not hate the Chinese. Please note, Chairman Mao. There is much that divides the two peoples, but there are fine qualities which they share.

I had quizzed Pastor Wang about the formation of the American Board of the Chinese Overseas Christian Mission. In 1959, Pastor Wang went to the States and met Dr. John Leighton Stewart, former American Ambassador to China, a trusted friend whom I have already mentioned.

"Have the English helped you very much financially?" he asked. When the Pastor replied, "Not much", which was true at the time, he asked, "Why not us?" He introduced Pastor Wang to influential church leaders.

On that visit he stayed in a guest house where the manageress was a Miss I. Gale who suggested that he should meet Dr. Donald T. McIntosh, a Methodist minister who was staying there that night. Dr. McIntosh had been visiting a New York specialist about his hearing, but he left early next morning before the introductions were made.

Pastor Wang went on to Baltimore, where he stayed with Dr. and Mrs. Frederick M. Pyke whose family had worked in China for three generations.

"Do you know Dr. McIntosh?" he asked.

"We do indeed. If you'd like to meet him let's invite him to a meal."

That meeting was to prove a turning point, for Dr. McIntosh quickly saw the immense possibilities of winning Chinese for Christ during their exile from home. He told about himself. He and his brother-in-law had been playing golf when there was a sudden thunderstorm. They hurried to a small hut for shelter, but a thunderbolt struck them, killing his brother-in-law, and making his own hearing problem more acute. But the thunderbolt also awakened in him a desire to live more effectively.

He was the minister of a Methodist church in Maryland where, following the example of Dr. Oswald J. Smith of Toronto, whom he had heard preach, he commenced a missionary week. When he fixed the missionary target at eight thousand dollars he was told it was absurd in view of the resources and size of the church, but he prayed and planned, invited speakers, and during the week twelve thousand dollars were promised. The target was increased annually and when he left the church the year's missionary giving was twenty-five thousand dollars. After a further five years of ministry in Washington, D.C., he left the pastorate and received a special appointment to become the director of the C.O.C.M. American board. His wife, Evelyn, gifted as artist and musician, is secretary.

Dr. Stuart's influence was considerable in forming the American Board with the help of Dr. and Mrs. Fred Pyke and their son Dr. James Pyke, of Wesley Theological Seminary. On my first American trip I met the Pykes and renewed fellowship with Dr. and Mrs. McIntosh, whom I had met in 1962 in London. It was obvious how much the mission owed to them.

It was not until I arrived there that I discovered the extent of my schedule, or how much an American packs into a day. On the Sunday morning I had to preach in a Methodist church at Poolsville, Maryland. Before the service I slumped to my knees and confessed to God my inadequacy. Standing in the pulpit of a large church, facing a mixed congregation including influential business leaders, was quite different from leading a nurses' Bible study. I was incapable of expressing all I wished, but I told the story of our church in London, and of God's protecting hand upon my family. The congregation responded, which gave me confidence. For three months I travelled, preached and lectured, and soon found myself using Americanisms, but I seldom saw Pastor Wang whom I had originally thought would be travelling with me.

"Mary, why are you not working full-time for the mission?" several people asked.

"I am a nurse, I have passed my examinations: the hospital supplies my needs and I give my free time to the mission which anyhow is not in a position to support me."

Long days, late nights, overflowing hospitality, a tight schedule, always talking or sightseeing, I began to be a little dazed, and even more so when towards the end of the tour a group of generous friends approached me.

"Mary, we want to send you back to England as our missionary among the Chinese. We will undertake financial responsibility for you to the C.O.C.M. We are burdened for the Chinese. We can no longer send our missionaries into your country, but we wish to share this new opportunity with you."

I was unsure of myself. It was a gesture characteristic of American Christians. I was unworthy, and in English was still apt to be lost for the right word. I was so overcome that I could not give an answer. So much had happened. It seemed only yesterday that I was a medical student in Shanghai.

I thought of the Cultural Revolution in China in which Chairman Mao was using the Red Guards to close the last of the Christian churches. What was happening to the Christians in Shanghai with whom I had worshipped, to those among whom I had grown up, to the medical students who were now doctors, to the pastors who had refused to compromise?

Neale Hunter, an Australian teacher who was in Shanghai at this time, has told in *China Observed* (Sphere Books) how religion was already in such a weak state that it came as a surprise when in August 1966 the Red Guards attacked it. "In the major cities, the clergy were ordered to return to their native villages, the religious buildings were shorn of any architectural and ornamental features which the Red Guards found objectionable, anti-religious propaganda was put up on the walls, and every church, mosque, temple and monastery was 'secularised'."

A Party Secretary at Mr. Hunter's Institute told them that the Constitution still guaranteed freedom of belief. "The Constitution stands," he declared. "Nothing has changed. There is still freedom of religion in China."

"Here," Mr. Hunter says, "he paused, knowing that the foreigners had seen the spires coming down, the red flags flying from religious buildings, the notices reviling believers as 'rolling eggs' and reactionaries of the worst kind. 'However,' he went on, 'there is also the freedom to oppose religion. This is a prerogative that cannot be denied to the people!'" The atmosphere of the meeting was so tense that none of the foreigners dared challenge him." Mr. Hunter adds: "The practice of religion has been stopped. This applies not only to creeds of foreign origin, such as Christianity, Islam and Buddhism, but also to the native Chinese products of Taoism and Confucianism."

With more than eight hundred million Chinese denied any religion, our responsibility in C.O.C.M. was immense. I contacted Pastor Wang.

"Pray about it, Mary," he said. "It is a very generous offer, but you must discover the will of God. Ultimately, nothing else matters."

So it came about that I decided to give up nursing to work among the Chinese nurses and to give whatever assistance I could to Pastor Wang, whose responsibilities were becoming international. The prospect of being on the staff of the mission was incredible, but first I had to see my hospital matron. She was not wholly pleased. I do not blame her.

"Isn't your first duty to the hospital?" she asked, when I sat in her office on my return to London. There was a need for nurses, a need which existed throughout Britain, but I had to explain that for me there were other loyalties. She listened patiently, and I think she understood for she made it possible for me not to have to work a month's notice, which I was willing to do, so I might begin my task.

There were hundreds of Chinese nurses throughout the country. For a start Pastor Wang wrote to hospitals in and around London telling of my appointment and asking for a list of Chinese nurses on the staff. Matrons, with few exceptions, were encouraging in their replies. Chinese girls accounted for as much as sixty to seventy per cent of the student nurses in some hospitals, and few had less than twenty Chinese girls. They came direct from Hong Kong, Malaysia, and Singapore, each having made individual application and having paid their own fare. From the airport they went directly to the hospital, many knowing no one except the name of the matron with whom they had corresponded.

Most were able to read and write better than they could speak English, as matrons soon discovered. They had had a secondary education, and were between eighteen and twenty-one. A few, from wealthy families, were able to return home for holidays, but the majority would not see their parents until they completed their training. Usually, they planned to return home permanently when they had qualified. A few had attended meetings of the Nurses' Christian Fellowship which was founded in 1942 to unite nurses who desire to witness for Christ: to bring nurses to a saving knowledge of Jesus Christ: to deepen the spiritual life of all members of the Fellowship especially by means of prayer and Bible study: and to encourage missionary interest and activity at home and abroad.

Chinese nurses, bound by a labour permit, having crossed the world to qualify, try very hard to overcome difficulties and stick to nursing. They experience the same frustrations as English girls, and an equal weariness at the end of a foot-weary shift, plus acute homesickness on occasions. Although tradition is changing fast, in the East a girl there still tends to be closely sheltered within the family. Arriving in London, or some provincial city, with no friends and language difficulties, it was easy to panic or to retreat from social contact.

I found my task greater than I or the C.O.C.M., or my American supporters, had visualised. I soon had the names of 1,200 girls out of an estimated 2,000 in Britain. Today there are more than 4,000. I visited hospitals, making appointments with nurses and senior staff, even attempting to write to the girls, only to discover the more I did the greater the demand. Opportunities to address groups of Christian nurses multiplied, but my call was to my own people so I had to discipline myself. God gave me encouragement in that first year.

Loneliness was a problem, no one was to blame and

there was no easy solution. Girls with extrovert personalities, gay, talkative, mixed with the English girls, but the entirely different cultural backgrounds resulted in numerous probationers retreating to their own rooms where they stayed until the next duty period. They had no life outside their class or ward and, without stimulating interests, tiredness resulted in depression. When Chinese nurses did congregate together hospital authorities frowned, not least because their command of English did not improve when they moved only among themselves.

About five per cent of the girls were Christians, but I was in the midst of a growing missionary situation and many were responsive. A large percentage on arrival, when asked their religion, would state Buddhist, and this was noted in their personal file, but it was frequently the nominal religion of their parents or grandparents. There was no personal adherence. There is a Chinese proverb 'Three ways to one goal', suggesting that Buddhism, Taoism and Confucianism are each philosophies showing the direction of life. I said there was one way to the goal — and that the way was Jesus Christ, who said: 'I am the Way, the Truth and the Life, no man cometh unto the Father but by Me.' Matrons, understandably, did not wish to influence the religion or philosophy of the girls, and in isolated cases knowing they were Buddhists were reluctant to give me their names. The hospital, they explained, had a chaplain to whom they could go if in need. Few did. Gradually, we were to gain the confidence of most hospital authorities for they found our genuine concern for the total welfare of their staff. A nurse can be frighteningly lonely or homesick whether she is a Christian or a Buddhist, and in Christ's name we offered friendship.

Our first contact in a hospital was often with a Christian girl, but soon without encouragement others were seeking advice, including those who had been told by their parents:

"Now we hear England is a Christian country. We are sending you there to do your nursing and to do well, and you will return with your diplomas and certificates, and your status will be recognised, but remember we are Buddhists."

The family may dislike Christianity because their picture of Christ is confused with empire-building: gun-boats and commercial exploitation. The Lord Jesus of the New Testament, God incarnate, who allowed no barriers of colour or class, is unknown to them. It is hardly their fault if they see Christianity as a western religion. They have not grasped that Christ was born in neither London nor New York, and that He came to save the world.

Chinese girls were startled by the hours they spent on ward duty compared with in the classroom. They had visualised the reverse. The Chinese worship education and think of it in terms of books and lectures rather than making beds and taking temperatures. After eight hours, up and down the wards, coping with admissions, emptying bedpans, maintaining a marvellous calm on the hospital treadmill, they returned to their rooms dog-tired, wishing only to rest their feet. Which is not to quarrel with the system, for after three years on a busy ward, involved in a variety of duties and crises and living with suffering, a nurse knows almost by instinct how to cope. Most relish it, absorbing knowledge on the job, rarely permitting the luxury of reflection but involved with patients whose trusting eyes follow their comings and goings. Such a nurse is welcome almost anywhere in the world.

"Matron is very strict," I was told, especially about the older matrons, who remembered how they were treated when they first entered the profession. I had a tutor who believed in firm discipline, but attitudes were changing. Those who were taught to speak to matron with eyes down, in tones of deep respect, may not approve, but too much severity makes nurses scared of making an approach when they should.

I was immersed in their personal problems, from language to relationships, and had to ask myself what proportion of time I should give to them. I was not a social worker but people cannot be compartmentalised and I found myself spending hours talking with those who had failed examinations, who had aggressive attitudes towards a senior staff nurse or sister, who questioned if they were in the right profession, or found the long hours a burden. Some were troubled by so much suffering, or were themselves sick, or were in distress over news from home.

When I had sane advice I gave it, but I learned that by listening I could also ease the pressures. I told how God had led me, step by step, event by event, from home to Shanghai, from there to Hong Kong, and eventually to London; how I also had faced difficulties in training as a nurse and study of English. Their problems were genuine. Sometimes I knew the solution; for example when it was wise for a nurse to be transferred to another hospital, but if this involved a senior member of staff, it presented obstacles which kept me awake at night.

My correspondence grew. "Let us ask Mary Wang to come." I had no secretary at the beginning and often the girl could not be seen until she came off duty at 8 p.m. I spent the mornings writing letters, the afternoons seeing girls who could call, and the evenings visiting nurses' homes. I was engaged in a great adventure, abundantly worthwhile, and was so grateful to the American friends who were supporting me, but I was in danger of spreading myself too much.

I received friendship as well as giving it. Often those to whom I ministered out of my weakness gave me support. In a country hospital near St. Albans I met Mary Fu, and was immediately drawn by her loving personality. Her father was a sailor and her mother had a business in Hong Kong, but she was experiencing difficulties with her English studies and this was hindering her training. It was suggested that she change her course, but instead she resigned from the hospital and for a time lived in our Chinese centre. There is one room which can sleep five, and normally there were several girls spending a few nights or a week there. Mary Fu remained three weeks and became a Christian.

I was so happy. We had long talks about her future and I approached the matron of the Brompton hospital who accepted her for training as a state enrolled nurse rather than, as previously, for the more taxing state registered nursing course. On her days off she returned to our centre doing voluntary office work, filing, addressing envelopes, answering the telephone, making refreshments, proving herself to be quick and efficient.

Mary Fu's conversion was never in doubt, but as her training at Brompton continued I became concerned for her. Occasionally, I would be able to spend a little time with her and we would pray together; she began to lose weight and the doctor diagnosed a tumour in the thyroid. She was admitted to another London hospital for an operation.

In the afternoon on the day of the operation she was dangerously ill. Did I know where her father could be reached? She had told me that he was with Blue Funnel and the London office found that he was in Singapore, and a message was radioed asking him to come to London.

Mary Fu fought for her life. After the operation she was sent back to the ward but started to choke on recovering from the anaesthetic. She was hurried back to theatre, a journey involving a lift, and on the way her heart stopped. She was resuscitated but remained unconscious, and when her condition worsened she was moved to an intensive care unit at another hospital.

She was an only child and when I met her father on his arrival I shared his gloom.

"Miss Wang," he said, "I just don't understand why this should happen to my daughter." She had written to tell her parents of her faith, but that added to his bewilderment as he saw her lying unconscious week after week. The hospital provided a room in which he slept.

"There are many things we don't understand," I said. "Please allow me to pray with you."

Humanly speaking there was no hope, but our members were praying. Pastor Wang made his way almost directly to the hospital on his return from South Africa; we put on gowns and masks and went into the unit where her life was in the balance.

"Mary," I said, "it's Pastor Wang back from South Africa."

She started crying as if she had understood.

"I'm going to pray for you," he said.

From that day she slowly began to recover. She had been unconscious eight weeks, and had lost her speech, but her father lovingly nursed and fed her. Eventually, she was able to commence speech therapy, so that she can now talk freely.

While dangerously ill she had a vivid dream which she will not forget. She was on a tossing sea, in a coffin, and the lid was being nailed down. She wanted to object, to say "I am not dead yet", but the words would not come. She told me, "While they were hammering I heard someone say, 'Stop'. I realised it was your voice, Mary, and you came and took off the lid. You pulled me up and said, 'Come with me'. From that dream I began to think for myself and to cry to God. It was the hour when I became conscious of myself again."

139

Mary Fu's mother has travelled to England to be with her daughter, and although Mary may never return to nursing, her faith has held.

"Mother," she said, "without Jesus you would not have me today. God brought me back to life and I am still in His care. I can't be a nurse, but I am not bitter and I will learn to be patient."

Mary is one of more than a hundred nurses who have become Christians through this ministry. Her courage presents a challenge to me.

Janet from Kuala Lumpur, Malaysia, stayed in the centre for two weeks before commencing her hospital training. She became a Christian on Pastor Wang's birthday during her stay with us. I took her to the hospital in my car on the day she started training and afterwards she wrote: "I felt an unspeakable joy when I put on my uniform for the first time, realising that the Lord has brought me here from such a far country that I may be led to His saving knowledge. I wish that I shall be kept by Him and shall never go astray. I promise that I shall read my Bible and pray every day."

Today, in the nurse's work I have the assistance of Miss Kwei Lan Liew. She is younger than I, nearer the age of many of the girls in training, and her gay, lively personality wins quick acceptance. Her appointment came about when I spent three months in America in the autumn, 1968. I mentioned Kwei Lan as someone who might be able to assist me, but added that I had hesitations because she had only been converted that spring. As I had counselled her about the Christian life she had shared my burden and I found her very responsive for one so new in the faith. She was in her final year at the King Edward Memorial hospital at Ealing, where I had trained, and staff and patients had seen the change in her.

While I thought of her and prayed for her during my

American visit, in London, unknown to me, God was speaking to her. She wanted others to share this life-changing experience, particularly the nurses whom she understood and loved. She believed that God was calling her to work with C.O.C.M.

Dr. and Mrs. McIntosh promised to find financial support for a colleague for me, saying that an associate would free me to travel more on behalf of the mission. As I was reading my Bible and preparing for an evening service I suddenly felt compelled to write to Kwei Lan asking how she would feel about joining me.

As my letter went by air to London I received a letter from her: possibly, somewhere over the sea they had crossed. She told how the challenge had come to her. At first she considered it impossible. She came from a non-Christian family and had intended returning to her parents and younger brothers and sisters on completion of her training. But God was asking: "Are you willing to serve Me?"

Her letter was confirmation that my leading had been right, and in January 1969, she was appointed my assistant, since when she has led many into faith giving herself unsparingly, and nurses who may have been reserved with me have opened their hearts to her.

In the office, since 1968, we have been blessed with Maylee Doa, a Chinese girl from India, who took her nurse's training in Manchester where she became active in our fellowship there. I met her in 1967 when I was speaking there and on a second visit I stayed with her when I learned that before her nurse's training she had been a secretary for a Japanese company in India. I met her a third time at a weekend house-party in Wales and told her about our need in London.

"Is it easy to work with Pastor Wang?" she asked.

"No, not very," I laughed, "but I'd rather work with him than anyone."

12

JUNE 20, 1964, was a day of rejoicing. Bishop Frank Houghton opened and dedicated the Chinese Church Centre, in Hollywood Road, London, purchased for £10,000, excluding the furnishing and fitting. Gifts had come from many countries including the American branch of the C.O.C.M. Church services continued in the Central Y.M.CA. but we regarded the centre with its facilities for fellowship almost as 'Chinese soil'. Pastor Wang made his home there, and within two weeks there were three conversions.

The doctrinal basis was Evangelical. In formal language: We believe in the divine inspiration of the Holy Scriptures as authority in matters of faith and conduct. The unity of the Father, the Son and the Holy Spirit in the Godhead. The universal sinfulness and guilt of human nature. Redemption from the guilt, penalty and power of sin only through the sacrificial death of Jesus Christ the Incarnate Son of God. The resurrection of Jesus Christ from the dead. The necessity of the work of the Holy Spirit to make the death of Christ effective to the individual sinner, granting him repentance towards God and faith in Jesus Christ. The indwelling and work of the Holy Spirit in the believer. The expectation of the personal return of the Lord Jesus.

Those who differed in their theology were welcome to worship with us, but this basis was maintained in the ministry. Pastor Wang preached in Mandarin and there was simultaneous translation into English. There were services in Cantonese for those from Hong Kong.

In 1965 Operation Mobilisation arranged a day's

training course, after which for a week three teams went forth from the centre with books for sale and tracts for free distribution among Chinese families scattered throughout London. Thousands of tracts were used, several hundred books sold, and there was a good response to the meetings on the Friday and Saturday evenings.

A medical doctor in Dublin, Y. F. Ng, became a Christian through reading a tract given him by one of our members.

Mary Seow came from a Buddhist family in Malaysia. When she left home she was given a charm to carry, with the belief that it would bring her luck and success. We met her on a visit to Chase Farm hospital, Enfield, and talked with her about the Lord Jesus. She did not make her decision right away, but was willing to think it over. In the following week, when she was facing an important examination, she put aside her charm and prayed. God honoured her faith. She became a Christian and started to rejoice in Bible study and prayer.

Each autumn Friendship Campaigns were held for those arriving from South-East Asia for the university and college courses commencing in late September or early October. Names, where possible, were obtained from the British Council, the Inter-Varsity Fellowship, and local authorities, and incoming flights were met. Young people were organised into teams, students on vacation giving up to four weeks. A few came by ship, but most arrived on charter flights at Gatwick and Stansted airports. There were coffee evenings, films, musical concerts, and always an invitation to our church.

In 1971 there are sixty thousand Chinese in Britain, thirty thousand of them in London, a large percentage being students, nurses or restaurant staff. Those in restaurants are the responsibility of Mr. Frank Cheung who sold his restaurant in Birmingham to concentrate on visiting the two thousand plus Chinese establishments in Britain. In the first nine months he talked with more than seven hundred people. Mr. Cheung says: "The work among these restaurant people is like an undeveloped plot of land which needs tears to irrigate and diligent labour to plough, before the seeds of the Gospel can be sown."

Thomas Heng, now back in Malaysia, in his booklet about the Chinese church, commented that young people formed a majority of the congregation.

"A visitor to the church services would inevitably notice the youthfulness (as compared with the British churches) of the congregation. On any Sunday, one might expect to find some seventy per cent of the congregation under the age of twenty-five; some twenty-five per cent between the ages of twenty-six and fifty; and only about five per cent who have lived half a century. Of the under twenty-fives, only two per cent have not reached the age of fifteen (this does not include the Sunday school). In other words the Chinese church is predominantly a church of people between the ages of sixteen and twenty-five. Most are university or college students, articled clerks, nurses or graduate students. Some who have completed their courses are 'freshers' to their professions, but lack the experience which comes with years of work. The young character of the church presents some problems."

He went on: "The Chinese church has become the spiritual birthplace and training ground for innumerable Chinese doctors, teachers, lawyers, accountants, nurses, and secretaries who today serve in countries such as Hong Kong, Taiwan, Malaysia, Singapore, Mauritius, Canada and the United States of America. Recently in Hong Kong at a gathering of fifteen friends who had been studying in England, twelve indicated that they were brought to a saving knowledge of Jesus Christ at the London Chinese church."

Pastor Wang received a Christmas card from Hong Kong which said: "Perhaps you would like to know that all the former Chinese church folks in Hong Kong are engaged in active service for the Lord."

We know of more than 1,500 who have found Christ in our fellowship, and in the last year there have been 118 conversions and thirty baptisms.

Thomas Heng described three problems which face the church. First, because of its youthful character, the inexperience of members in matters secular and spiritual, there has been a great deal of trial and error. Experience would have saved heartache. Secondly, there is the highly flexible nature of the membership. "Being temporary residents in the country, some staying two or three years while others for perhaps four or five, a large proportion of the congregation is constantly changing. This rapid turnover of the congregation inevitably affects the stability and continuity of organisation and work."

The third area of difficulty he mentions is finance, so many members being students.

Our youthfulness is emphasised by the fact that during the first twenty years we had only one funeral service, that of Mrs. Fan who died in 1970. She was the foundation member in whose home the first services were held.

Members are encouraged to attend a local church on Sunday mornings, and in at least two London churches there is a Chinese colony. Our activities are in the afternoon and evening.

Until 1965 it was possible to send the communion service offerings through Hong Kong to Christians in the mainland. Now we remind ourselves of those who remain there by often singing a hymn from China. The words came to us in a letter acknowledging a gift. We use them in the church and they hang on a wall of my home, headed 'A Hymn from China'. Here is an English translation:

I think of Thee night and day, Jesus.
What are sinners Thou shouldest save?
My foolish heart Thy righteous path now walks
And runs straight ahead toward the goal,
All my love now before Thy feet I pour;
As dung everything I count.
Nothing more do I long for in heaven or earth,
Though tears come but I shall press on.

I'll praise Thee always night and day, Jesus.
What are sinners Thou shouldest care?
Thy love is unchanging as the hills,
And Thy promise strong as shields.
All my blood now before Thy feet Lord, I pour,
Thou King of kings, Lord of lords.
Thy Word which I trust may Thou keep, Jesus.
When death comes I shall find my peace.

Because so little news comes from Communist China
there is a danger that the church there may be forgotten.
Never was prayer more needed. We adapt the prayer of the
Apostle Paul in Romans 10: 1: 'Brethren, my heart's desire
and prayer to God for China is that they might be
saved.'

More than one fourth of the world's population is Chinese, but the Chinese, including those in the free world, are
a frightened people. They know not where the next test
will come. They have run to Hong Kong, Indonesia, India,
to almost every country, but they cannot find security. In
parts of India and Malaysia they have been persecuted.
Real security is found only in God and nowhere else. Because the Chinese know the plight of the world they have
often shown a readiness to turn to Christ.

To possess a Bible in China is to risk imprisonment or
death. The Bible House in Shanghai remained open for

several years after the Communist takeover, and I purchased Bibles there, but even then possession marked one out. During my indoctrination in college my Bible was taken away as I found comfort in its pages, and this was considered a hindrance. They apologised when they took it away and it was later returned, but during the weeks without it I found strength in those passages which I had memorised.

The C.O.C.M. today places emphasis on the importance of memorising or, in the Psalmist's words, hiding God's word in the heart so that we can meditate upon it while walking alone, in bed, while washing, in any place. If there comes a day when public worship is forbidden and there are no Bibles, it is the Scriptures we have memorised which will keep the faith pure.

In 1968, on my second tour in America, this time by myself, I spoke twice at the Pentagon to senior army staff and their wives. A general presented me with a glorious Chinese dress which had belonged to a dowager in Peking. It was exquisitely embroidered, and very valuable, but he explained that he did not think it should be in the possession of an American. I gave it to a trusted friend.

In 1969 Dr. McIntosh left his church to become Executive Director in America of C.O.C.M. Dr. Pyke and Dr. McIntosh that year arranged eleven banquets at which I presented the aims of the Mission. For our new centre, in London, to be opened in the seventies, we needed £75,000. £15,000 had been pledged by the summer of 1969, and during my American visit a further £20,000 was pledged.

Pastor Wang's vision was worldwide. The Chinese were everywhere. As a result of the labours of Mr. and Mrs. H. W. Pudney, a Chinese Baptist church was opened in Johannesburg with the Reverend Arthur Song, a South African born Chinese, trained in the Johannesburg Baptist

Bible college, as pastor. Pastor Wang spent six weeks in South Africa holding meetings for the Chinese and saw the formation of the Chinese Christian Fellowship in Cape-town.

In Paris the congregation has grown. One remarkable conversion was that of a Chinese businessman, which occurred in Moscow while he was returning to France from a business journey to mainland China. When faced with serious problems he prayed to God, about whom he had heard Pastor Wang speak. His prayer was answered. With repentance and deep thanksgiving on landing in Paris he sought out the Chinese Christians.

In 1970 Mr. Harry Hughes became deputation secretary for the C.O.C.M. and pastor of the Manchester Chinese Christian Fellowship. When our fellowship was established in Manchester in 1966 he was a local representative of the Overseas Missionary Fellowship and so was invited to be an adviser to our fellowship. He attended our summer conference at Ashburnham, with his family, and heard God's call. He knew no Chinese and was not Chinese, but Pastor Wang gladly welcomed him into C.O.C.M. and he is greatly loved by the Chinese. The ministry in Manchester was primarily among students, but now it has spread to residents, and there is a Chinese Sunday school with more than fifty children.

A group of former members of the London church and other fellowships were meeting on Sunday mornings in Singapore. In Canada a C.O.C.M. group had been formed, under the leadership of Mr. C. K. Seow. The work in Holland, mainly centred in the Hague, Amsterdam and Rotterdam progressed. The church in Paris has now purchased new premises, and the Reverend John Lu has been appointed director for Australia and New Zealand.

My parents retired from their ministry in Hong Kong in March 1968, and were given permission to make their residence in Britain. As father was as strong as ever, physically and spiritually, it had been a job to persuade him to retire. I wrote: "Father, if you don't retire, it will be difficult for younger men to step in. You must give them a chance." We met mother and father at the airport and brought them to our London home: they could not get over the fact that they were in Europe. A Pastor was needed for the Chinese church in Paris, and father accepted the invitation from the church and the C.O.C.M. to be its pastor during 1969.

While I was still nursing, in November 1965, Martin came from Hong Kong to work with a London firm of architects. I was glad to welcome him. I will never forget how when I was studying at medical school and he was in north China he shared his income equally with me. In February 1966, he married Martha Lee, a nurse, to whom he had been engaged for several years. I have been living with them since just like a Chinese family and our parents have been with us since their return from Paris. We all wanted to provide a home for Pastor Wang and so he also joined us and became another grandpa to Martin's children. As we had the same surname many thought that he and my father were brothers.

My brother Michael and my sister Ruby remain in Hong Kong, both happily married. Michael is an engineer, Ruby, a teacher. For several years she assisted father as a pianist and a Sunday school teacher.

In 1970 Pastor Wang underwent two major operations. An X-ray the previous year had shown a stomach ulcer. He was taken into hospital on Sunday, April 12 for investigations. Earlier the doctor, knowing he did not take holidays and that his work involved emotional and mental strain had ordered him to ease up, to rest whenever possible, and take the medicine prescribed. I was in the States which made it difficult for him to rest. On my return, finding there was no improvement, I talked with the doctor.

"Pastor Wang must have complete rest," he told me. "He must leave his work entirely for a period."

"If I tell him doctor, he won't believe me," I said. So the doctor wrote him a note. During January and February he mainly stayed in bed, but a constant stream of young people called to see him. In March, there was little improvement, so one of our doctor members arranged for him to see a specialist. His own doctor gave permission for this and an appointment was made. While I was in the States, because of his age and the persistent symptoms, he was admitted to hospital. His heart condition was good and it was decided to operate. It was a major operation but as I was travelling in America, moving from place to place with Dr. and Mrs. McIntosh, the mails did not reach me.

A cable was sent to Toronto, two days before his operation, suggesting I return if the remainder of my programme were not important. I did not receive it and Dr. Pyke tried to trace me without success. After the operation a second cable was sent. I was eventually contacted by telephone by the Pykes. I telephoned London and the hospital said he had had a haemorrhage, so I caught the first flight next morning via New York. I was very upset but the stewards were most kind offering me food and drink. I refused, wanting to fast and pray. A French steward saw my state and said, "I am so sorry Madam. Is there anything I can do for you?"

"Are you a Christian?" I asked. "Do you pray?"

"I am a Roman Catholic." He promised to pray.

Martin, now an architect in London, met me at Heathrow, at eleven on the night of the 21st. We telephoned the hospital which said that Pastor was seriously ill. When we arrived there at midnight I told the night porter: "I would like to see Pastor Wang."

"Nobody is allowed to go up to the ward at this hour," he said.

"May I please see the night superintendent?" I asked.

When the sister came she said: "Are you Miss Wang from the States? Come with me."

We walked along the long corridor which went under the road and lead to University College hospital, where a nurse took me to his bedside. I looked at his face and although he was asleep I knew his condition was critical. I remained by his bed silently crying, and the nurse who kept returning to take his blood pressure wept with me. When Pastor opened his eyes I said softly, "It's Mary here. I'm back."

"Mary, you're back. When did you come?"

"Uncle, many are praying for you. You will be all right."

The night superintendent came and advised me to leave. "He is happier now that you are back," she said. "Return in the morning."

From then they allowed me to stay with him whenever I wished. He began to improve and was able to sit in a chair. There was still an obstruction and the blood drip had to accompany him but I remember he was strong enough to sit in the T.V. room with other patients. "Why do you look so depressed and unhappy," he asked a middle-aged lady and was able to comfort her.

I spent the mornings in the office attending to the mail and routine, then each day after a quick lunch I went to the hospital staying until nine or ten in the evening.

On May 2 he had a second operation. Medically, I was told, he stood little chance and our faith was tested, "Lord, if you see fit give him a few more years to continue the work," we begged. One young man prayed: "If it is possible make us suffer and so lessen his suffering. We have strong bodies and can endure it but he is so weak."

"God can you ignore such a prayer?" I pleaded.

I regretted my medical training when he was so seriously ill because the doctors could not keep the truth from me. Five days after the second operation his liver had almost stopped functioning and he became jaundiced. Permission was sought from the matron's office for me to stay the night. My assistant was with me. Pastor had a high fever, but was not allowed a drop of water. When available he could rinse his mouth with iced water. Towards twelve-thirty the night superintendent suggested that one of us should go home and rest. Pastor asked me to stay. I knew that many patients died between one and four.

"Mary," Pastor said to me about three, "I am weaker and weaker. I do not think there is any hope but I have peace in my heart."

I found it almost impossible to control my tears.

"Uncle, so many are praying for you."

He was too weak to continue talking. He closed his eyes and softly I began to sing. Young people from the church had sung to him earlier and it had strengthened him.

We had sent out a letter to those on our mailing list requesting prayer and this was read at the London May meeting of the Overseas Missionary Fellowship.

On May 17 he began to improve, and we believed that God had touched his body. He was still taking nothing by mouth and the specialist said that as an obstruction remained a third operation was necessary. The Pastor refused.

"There is no need for another operation," he said. "The Lord has touched me with His hand."

The specialist took me outside. "Let me tell you Miss Wang," he said, "that his condition will force me to operate."

Pastor, so grateful for what had been done for him, asked for an X-ray.

The specialist agreed.

"If there is still an obstruction then you may operate," Pastor said.

The X-ray revealed the obstruction had gone.

"You win," the specialist smiled.

"I did not win," Pastor said, "but God has blessed your earlier operations."

Long months of convalescence followed, in which Pastor shared with us his vision for the future, including a training school in London for young people who had completed their professional courses and were about to return to Asia. Our members born outside China should forever remember that as they were Chinese they had a Christian responsibility for China.

"We do not know when the door into China may open. When the day comes Chinese Christians must be ready to go in. I want our young people after gaining their qualifications to remain in London for up to six months to be trained in Bible study and personal evangelism; they should live in a community, in the mornings studying together and in the afternoons visiting among the Chinese. We need a building for this purpose."

Both a building fund and a scholarship fund were launched.

In February 1971, a secondary cancer affected his liver. He was undisturbed by the thought of death.

"You have been with me so many years," he said. "You cannot do anything of your own effort and strength but I want you to gather these workers like a family and carry on the work together. God called me when I was fifty years of age — none of you has reached that time yet, and therefore you have a much longer time if God allows, and therefore it is only right for God to expect more work to be done by you."

In the last two weeks of his life he was asked about his

154

earlier years. "Why do you want to know?" he asked. "Oh, perhaps one day we may want to write the life story of the founder." "Well, you may say: 'Stephen Wang: Past — obscure'. The first fifty years of my life are almost not worth talking about." Thus concluded the man who was at one time the principal of a college in north China, who had among his close associates the ambassadors of an earlier generation. Wherefore he determined to know nothing among them save Christ Jesus and Him crucified. Like Paul what things were gain to him he counted as loss for the sake of Christ. The man who had lived seventy years only reckoned those which he used fully to serve the Lord as meaningful and worthwhile.

On Sunday, March 14, scores of young people from the church came to his bedside to say goodbye. Afterwards they had a quiet prayer meeting in the adjacent room. He died on March 15, 1971, at 9.37 a.m. At nine-thirty I called several others to his bedside — Maylee, Kwei-Lan, Kah-Thuan and Frank Cheung. We prayed, thanking God for the privilege of serving with him. We re-dedicated our lives asking that we might be strengthened to press steadfastly on with what the Pastor had pioneered.

The funeral service was held in the Talbot Tabernacle. Pastor John Husan, our assistant pastor, conducted the service. There were tributes including one from the Reverend F. A. J. Harding, C.O.C.M. treasurer, who had been Pastor's best friend for twenty-one years. "I am here to tell you what his friendship and love has done for me personally," he said. "To know him was to love him and to want to serve him and to support him through thick and thin. He had his private grief. Most of you know he was a political exile from his own country and that his dear ones in China were cut off from any fellowship with him. One day I saw his face suffused with grief. I told him I was so sorry I could not enter into this sorrow. He said: 'When this

EPILOGUE

I was speaking at a conference in Indianapolis, when an elderly American took me aside. "Mary, what I don't understand is that we have been sending missionaries to China for the last hundred years or so; we started schools, universities, hospitals and built churches, then when the Communists came they threw us out."

I am often asked Why?

Myra Roper in her valuable book *China — the Surprising Country* (Heinemann), tells of her visit to a community church in Shanghai in the early 1960's. After the service Mr. C. W. Lee, the preacher, told how he had worked overseas but had returned to China since the revolution. "The Christian church has always seemed to have an unfortunate association with western wars and big business," he told her. "The churches were inextricably bound up with U.S. foreign policy. Overseas, some missionary boards met to decide how best to fight Communist aggression in China; this was interference in our national affairs, but even the best missionaries could not see why they should not do this."

He went on to say that people were often Christians for what they got out of the Westerners, 'rice-Christians'; in return they had to conform to their ideas, adapt themselves to non-Chinese ways; they often went to church because in some way, it paid them to do so.

"Now," he said, "people come to this church because they want to — they have no axe to grind, no 'right' people to meet any more. They come for fellowship and Christian counsel. Once we were called in Chinese 'eaters of the foreign religion', now we are called 'Believers in Jesus Christ' and that is what we want."

I wonder what happened to Mr. Lee and his believers when the remaining churches were closed in Shanghai in 1966? Does he now understand why mission boards did not welcome the Communist takeover? The Communist claim that American imperialists used the Christian church for its aggression in China is untrue, but because of frequent repetition millions believe it. The men of God I knew were not puppets of any governments but servants of Christ.

Communism claimed that missionaries were the instruments of colonial expansion; that they used their resources to enslave Chinese Christians to assist them in their aggression; that they taught doctrines which were coloured by imperialist poison; that they corrupted young minds with reactionary propaganda, dominating and controlling the churches.

A Methodist missionary, the Reverend R. E. Kendall, in China from 1939 to 1951, wrote in *World Dominion* after his expulsion:

"We can only prevent the coming of Communism by redeeming the society in which the church exists, changing its injustice into justice, its inequality into fairness, its corruption into honest administration, its desperate poverty into a measure of security, its social and racial discrimination into cooperation and partnership, becoming the conscience of society. It is not possible for the church to withstand the onslaught of armed Communism, but is it not possible for the church to prevent such a deterioration of society that the situation is reached in which Communism is the only answer . . . If the church cannot do anything about society it cannot do anything about the coming of Communism."

Leslie Lyall, one of China's missionary statesmen, in his book *Red Sky at Night* has a remarkable chapter on Criticism and Self-Criticism. He says: "We confess to our

Chinese friends: that too many of us were guilty of preaching a diluted Christian Gospel: that too many of us remained grossly ignorant of your culture, literature and thought; that too many of us were reluctant to identify ourselves with you; that we were too possessive to allow your free development; that we were too preoccupied with our institutions and too little concerned with planting strong local churches; that we neglected to prepare you for the advent of a Communist government; that we were too unconcerned about social injustice and lacking in social concern; that we sadly neglected to provide you with adequate Christian literature.

"We are sure," he concludes, "there were many other faults, omissions and sins. But these we confess with deep sincerity. Perhaps one day — God willing — we will be permitted to make amends."

Mr. Lyall, Chinese Christians like myself, too, confess. We accepted too easily the three hundred denominations and sects, all calling themselves Christian, which the missionaries introduced. We were lax in our stewardship, too willing to receive assistance from overseas. During the Japanese occupation when missionaries were in concentration camps we learned to survive alone, but on their release we settled back and let them assume leadership. We did not always encourage our best men to become theologians; we accepted a western interpretation of Christ's teachings, not easily assimilated by the Chinese. We showed less devotion and were less single-minded than Communist soldiers. We knew the Parable of the Good Samaritan but neglected our neighbour by the wayside.

For decades Christians in the west prayed for China. Have they ceased? Pray for my country. The Chinese church will not die, but it is sorely wounded, limping on sticks in the shadows.

159